THE
UNDERGROUND
RAILROAD

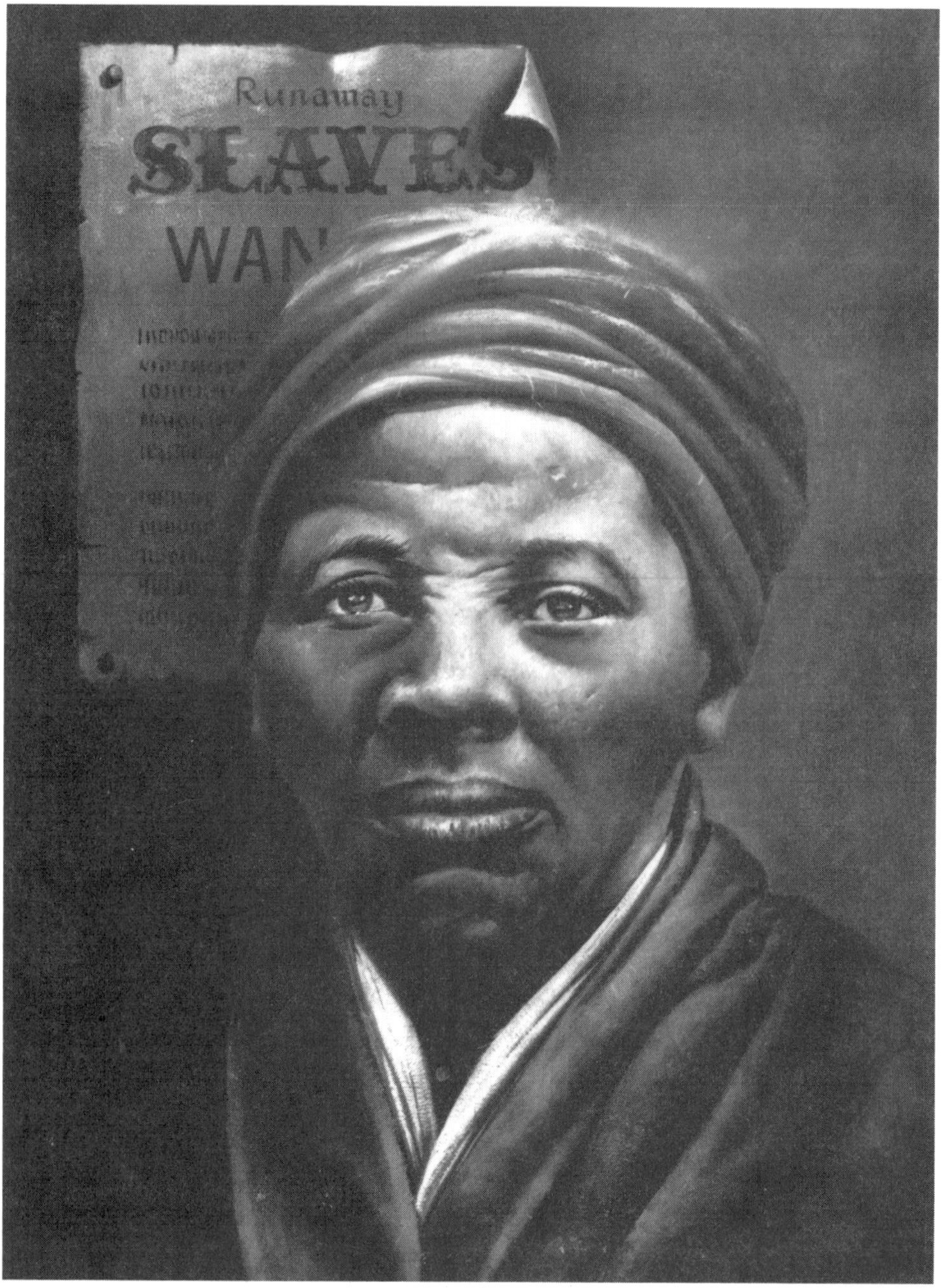
Runaway
SLAVES
WAN

The
UNDERGROUND
RAILROAD

SHAARON COSNER

Franklin Watts
New York / London / Toronto / Sydney / **1991**
A Venture Book

To Cynthia Lou Who

Frontispiece: Called the "Moses of her people," Harriet Tubman (circa 1820–1913) is perhaps the most well-known agent to have worked on the Underground Railroad.

Maps by Vantage Art, Inc.

Photographs copyright © : UPI/Bettmann Archives: pp. 2, 24, 28 inset, 61, 79 top, 80; New York Public Library, Picture Collection: pp. 12, 36, 37, 44, 56, 70, 77, 79 bottom, 107; New York Historical Society, N.Y.C.: p. 18; Brown Brothers: p. 29; Sophia Smith Collection, Smith College: p. 48

Library of Congress Cataloging-in-Publication Data
Cosner, Shaaron.
The underground railroad / by Shaaron Cosner.
p.   cm. – (A Venture book)
Includes bibliographical references and index.
Summary: Describes the underground railroad which helped slaves escape to freedom.
ISBN 0-531-12505-X
1. Underground railroad–Juvenile literature. 2. Fugitive slaves–United States–Juvenile literature. [1. Underground railroad. 2. Fugitive slaves.]   I. Title.
E450.C76   1991
973.7'115–dc20   91-18514   CIP   AC

CONTENTS

The runaway slave came to my house and stopt outside.
I heard his motions crackling the twigs of the woodpile,
through the swung half-door of the kitchen I saw him limpsy
*   and weak,*
And went where he sat on a log and led him and assured
*   him,*
And brought water and fill'd a tub for his sweated body and
*   bruis'd feet,*
And gave him a room that enter'd from my own, and gave
*   him some coarse clean clothes,*
And remembered perfectly well his revolving eyes and his
*   awkwardness,*
And remember putting plasters on the galls of his neck and
*   ankles;*
He stayed with me a week before he was recuperated and pass'd
*   north,*
I had him sit next to me at table, my fire-lock lean'd in
*   corner.*

—Walt Whitman,
Leaves of Grass

ONE
THE CONFLICT BEGINS

I always wanted to be free.
—Anthony Bingey, A slave from Missouri[1]

In 1794, a group of Quakers from Philadelphia helped one of George Washington's slaves to escape, and even the president of the United States dared not try to get his slave back. Washington wrote:

"The gentleman to whose care I sent him has promised every endeavor to apprehend him, but it is not easy to do this, when there are numbers who would rather facilitate the escape of slaves than apprehend them when run aways."[2]

ORIGINS OF SLAVERY

When the first slaves arrived in America at Jamestown, Virginia, in 1619, slavery was not new. Egyptians, Greeks, and Romans were among the societies that believed in slavery. Slavery on a large scale began in the fifteenth century when the Portuguese arrived in Africa and found that the African people lacked a stable government. This made it easy to take advantage of them. Besides, the slave traders reasoned, the Africans were not Christians and so it was acceptable to hold them in bondage. They also found that some Africans held other Africans as slaves and on this premise justified their slave trade.

Slavery became popular in the United States when a way of farming called the plantation system was developed. Slavery thrived on three conditions:

9

- a scarcity of labor
- the cultivation of certain types of crop that permitted the strict supervision of slaves using simple routines
- a low price for slaves

All of these conditions existed in the plantation system.

To grow tobacco, rice, sugarcane, and cotton, the young American colonies needed thousands of slaves to work the fields. The plantation owners had tried hiring Native American Indians, some of whom had held slaves themselves. But in Indian culture, women did most of the work and men who were put to work in the fields performed poorly. Also, Indians were not as easily intimidated as the blacks were. Unlike blacks, they were not strangers in a new land and they were not dazed by capture and a horrible trip across the ocean on a slave ship. Held in captivity, many Indians revolted, sickened, or even died from white people's diseases against which they had no immunity.

Plantation owners also tried using indentured servants, white men and women who agreed to work for a specified period of time. This arrangement was unsatisfactory because the indentured servants invariably left when their time of indenture ended. Many of them had been recruited from slums and jails and knew nothing about working in the fields. Some of the more cunning ran off before their time was out. Others had been apprenticed to a trade and were more suited to work in the city, not on a plantation.

The only solution to meet the great demand for laborers seemed to be to import African blacks, both from Africa and several of the Caribbean islands. These men and women could be brought over as indentured servants, but kept on for an unspecified period of time because they were not American citizens. They were used to working in the fields and highly vulnerable in a new country.

The second requirement for slavery—crops ideal for the strict supervision of slaves—was also present in the South. The soil and climate of the North were not conducive to raising crops such as sugar, rice, tobacco, and cotton, thus by and large leaving the South to develop an agricultural system. Although northern farms needed laborers, they did not require as many as the southern plantations did because they were smaller. Besides, northern farmers had a labor pool consisting of large numbers of immigrants to draw from.

The third criteria for slavery to exist—low prices for slaves—also existed in the South. As more and more slave ships arrived in southern ports with their human cargoes, the price of slave labor decreased. Throughout the seventeenth century, the climate in the South was right for the growth of slavery.

Many northeners did not agree that importing blacks as slaves was morally right. And they began very early to express their displeasure over this custom. As early as the 1600s, Richard Baxter, an Englishman living in the North warned:

> Remember that they are of as good a kind as you; that is, they are reasonable creatures as well as you, and born to as much liberty. If their sins have enslaved them to you, yet Nature made them your equals.[3]

Another time he warned:

> To go as Pirates and catch up poor Negros or People of another Land, that never forfeited Life or Liberty, and to make them slaves, and sell them, is one of the worst kind of Thievery in the world.[4]

LAWS ARE PASSED

Members of the northern legislatures agreed that slavery was wrong and began passing laws that made the institu-

tion of slavery illegal in their states. Vermont declared itself a free state in 1777. Others followed. Between 1780
and 1860, Ohio, Indiana, Illinois, Michigan, Wisconsin,
Pennsylvania, and Massachusetts all declared themselves
free. Sometimes a waiting period was established so that
not all existing slaves would be freed at once, but eventually, an African-American living or setting foot on
free state soil could live as a free American. (A map
tracing the progress of abolition and the slave trade is
found on pages 14–15.)

Canada, too, declared itself against slavery. Although
an act abolishing slavery in the colonies of England was
not passed until 1883, the parliament of Upper Canada
(now Ontario) passed a law against importing slaves in
1793 and said the children of slaves would become free at
the age of twenty-five. Slavery in Lower Canada (now
Quebec) was outlawed in 1800.

Southerners, for their part, moved quickly to enact
laws that would protect their valuable human property.
Laws against helping slaves escape were included in many
of the southern states' treaties and constitutions. Agree-
ments between colonists and Indians often contained a
clause for the return of escaped slaves.

In the late 1700s, even stricter laws, called fugitive
slave laws, were passed in the South. These laws stated
that a slave holder or even his agent or lawyer could seize
slaves when they escaped to another state. If the owner
was not present, an African-American could be arrested

A family of slaves poses shyly
for this photograph taken
around 1861 on a plantation
near Beaufort, South Carolina.

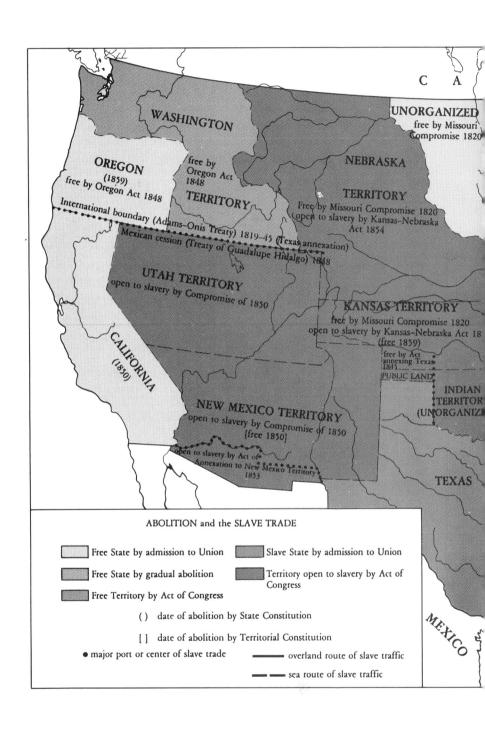

C   A

WASHINGTON

UNORGANIZED
free by Missouri
Compromise 1820

OREGON
(1859)
free by Oregon Act 1848

free by
Oregon Act
1848

TERRITORY

NEBRASKA

TERRITORY
Free by Missouri Compromise 1820
open to slavery by Kansas–Nebraska
Act 1854

International boundary (Adams–Onis Treaty) 1819–45 (Texas annexation)

Mexican cession (Treaty of Guadalupe Hidalgo) 1848

UTAH TERRITORY
open to slavery by Compromise of 1850

KANSAS TERRITORY
free by Missouri Compromise 1820
open to slavery by Kansas–Nebraska Act 18
(free 1859)

CALIFORNIA
(1850)

free by Act
annexing Texas
1845

PUBLIC LAND

NEW MEXICO TERRITORY
open to slavery by Compromise of 1850
[free 1850]

INDIAN
TERRITOR
(UNORGANIZE

open to slavery by Act of
Annexation to New Mexico Territory
1853

TEXAS

ABOLITION and the SLAVE TRADE

Free State by admission to Union

Slave State by admission to Union

Free State by gradual abolition

Territory open to slavery by Act of
Congress

Free Territory by Act of Congress

( )   date of abolition by State Constitution

[ ]   date of abolition by Territorial Constitution

● major port or center of slave trade   ——— overland route of slave traffic

— — sea route of slave traffic

MEXICO

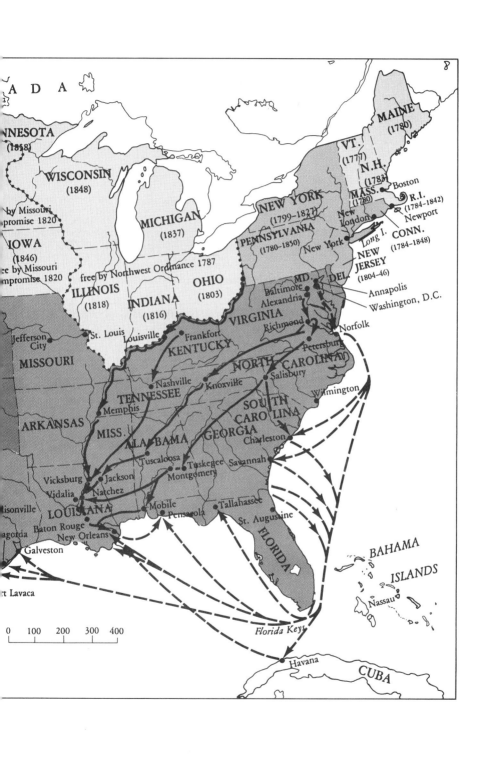

CANADA

MINNESOTA
(1858)

free by Missouri
Compromise 1820

IOWA
(1846)
free by Missouri
Compromise 1820

WISCONSIN
(1848)

MICHIGAN
(1837)

free by Northwest Ordinance 1787

ILLINOIS
(1818)

INDIANA
(1816)

OHIO
(1803)

MISSOURI

Jefferson
City

St. Louis

Louisville

Frankfort

KENTUCKY

Nashville

Knoxville

TENNESSEE

Memphis

ARKANSAS

MISS.

ALABAMA

Tuscaloosa

Tuskegee

Montgomery

GEORGIA

Vicksburg

Jackson

Vidalia

Natchez

Madisonville

LOUISIANA

Mobile

Pensacola

Tallahassee

Baton Rouge

New Orleans

St. Augustine

Galveston

FLORIDA

Port Lavaca

VIRGINIA

Richmond

NORTH CAROLINA

Salisbury

SOUTH
CAROLINA

Wilmington

Charleston

Savannah

NEW YORK
(1799–1827)

PENNSYLVANIA
(1780–1850)

New York

MAINE
(1780)

VT.
(1777)

N.H.
(1783)

MASS.
(1780)

Boston

R.I.
(1784–1842)

Newport

New
London

Long I.

CONN.
(1784–1848)

NEW
JERSEY
(1804–46)

MD.

DEL.

Baltimore

Alexandria

Petersburg

Norfolk

Annapolis

Washington, D.C.

BAHAMA
ISLANDS

Nassau

Florida Keys

Havana

CUBA

0   100   200   300   400

if he was even suspected of being a runaway unless he could produce evidence that he was free. If he could not produce the evidence and the authorities could not find out who his master was, they advertised in county newspapers. If no owner came forward, the slave was sold to the highest bidder and the money was used to pay the slave's jail fees and other expenses. The rest went into the county treasury.

REWARDS ARE OFFERED

Rewards were offered to those who would return an escaped slave. As early as 1699, Virginia officials offered "20 arms length of cloth" for any slave returned to his owner. [5]

Slave owners themselves offered rewards, and soon trees and walls were covered with signs offering money for the return of their "property":

TEN DOLLARS REWARD

RAN AWAY from the Subscriber on Saturday morning the 13th inst., A NEGRO WENCH named HAGAR, about five feet [1.52 m] high, thick set, had on a lindsey bed gown of blue and red, and a stuff petticoat of a brown colour and much worn, and a wool hat much worn. The above Reward will be given to any person for securing her in any jail, or delivering her to her master, near Budds' Ferry, Westmoreland County.

John Richey, Coppersmith [6]

HEAVY REWARD

TWO THOUSAND SIX HUNDRED DOLLARS REWARD. – Ran away from the subscriber on Saturday night, November 15th,

1856, Josiah and William Bailey and Peter Pennington. Joe is about 5 feet 10 inches [1.75 m] in height, of a chestnut color, bald head, with a remarkable scar on one of his cheeks, not positive on which it is, but think it is on the left, under the eye, has intelligent countenance, active, and well-made. He is about 28 years old. Bill is of a darker color, about 5 feet 8 inches in height, stammers a little when confused, well-made, and older than Joe, well-dressed, but may have pulled Kearsey on over their other clothes. Peter is smaller than either of the others, about 25 years of age, dark chestnut color, 5 feet 7 or 8. A reward of fifteen hundred dollars will be given to any person who will apprehend the said Joe Bailey, and lodge him safely in the jail at Easton Talbot Co., Md. and $300 for Bill and $800 for Peter.

W.R. Hughlett
John C. Henry
T. Wright[7]

WHY FREEDOM?

With so many people working to ensure that slaves remained in slavery, where could they run to? How could they escape? Why would they take the risk?

For some, freedom was an obsession. Others were forced to seek freedom, perhaps for fear they might be sold because their master had died or was getting too old to handle the plantation, or was in financial trouble. They knew that if they were sold they would be separated from their loved ones and so they escaped, hoping to return later for those they left behind. Or perhaps they wanted to escape the cruelty of the plantation system. As one slave, Christopher Nichols, said, "My master was killing me as fast as he could when I got away."[8]

HEWLETT & BRIGHT.

SALE OF

VALUABLE
SLAVES,

(On account of departure)

The Owner of the following named and valuable Slaves, being on the eve of departure for Europe, will cause the same to be offered for sale, at the NEW EXCHANGE, corner of St. Louis and Chartres streets, on *Saturday,* May 16, at Twelve o'Clock, *viz.*

1. **SARAH**, a mulatress, aged 45 years, a good cook and accustomed to house work in general, is an excellent and faithful nurse for sick persons, and in every respect a first rate character.

2. **DENNIS**, her son, a mulatto, aged 24 years, a first rate cook and steward for a vessel, having been in that capacity for many years on board one of the Mobile packets; is strictly honest, temperate, and a first rate subject.

3. **CHOLE**, a mulatress, aged 36 years, she is, without execption, one of the most competent servants in the country, a first rate washer and ironer, does up lace, a good cook, and for a bachelor who wishes a house-keeper she would be invaluable; she is also a good ladies' maid, having travelled to the North in that capacity.

4. **FANNY**, her daughter, a mulatress, aged 16 years, speaks French and English, is a superior hair-dresser, (pupil of Guilliac,) a good seamstress and ladies' maid, is smart, intelligent, and a first rate character.

5. **DANDRIDGE**, a mulatoo, aged 26 years, a first rate dining-room servant, a good painter and rough carpenter, and has but few equals for honesty and sobriety.

6. **NANCY**, his wife, aged about 24 years, a confidential house servant, good seamstress, mantuamaker and tailoress, a good cook, washer and ironer, etc.

7. **MARY ANN**, her child, a creole, aged 7 years, speaks French and English, is smart, active and intelligent.

8. **FANNY or FRANCES**, a mulatress, aged 22 years, is a first rate washer and ironer, good cook and house servant, and has an excellent character.

9. **EMMA**, an orphan, aged 10 or 11 years, speaks French and English, has been in the country 7 years, has been accustomed to waiting on table, sewing etc.; is intelligent and active.

10. **FRANK**, a mulatto, aged about 32 years speaks French and English, is a first rate hostler and coachman, understands perfectly well the management of horses, and is, in every respect, a first rate character, with the exception that he will occasionally drink, though not an habitual drunkard.

☞ All the above named Slaves are acclimated and excellent subjects; they were purchased by their present vendor many years ago, and will, therefore, be severally warranted against all vices and maladies prescribed by law, save and except FRANK, who is fully guaranteed in every other respect but the one above mentioned.

TERMS:—One-half Cash, and the other half in notes at Six months, drawn and endorsed to the satisfaction of the Vendor, with special mortgage on the Slaves until final payment. The Acts of Sale to be passed before WILLIAM BOSWELL, *Notary Public*, at the expense of the Purchaser.

New-Orleans, May 13, 1835.

Whatever their reasons for seeking freedom and regardless of the harsh conditions they would have had to survive in order to be free, many escaped slaves were prepared to die rather than go back to a life of slavery. On a chilly night in January 1856, for instance, a group of seventeen slaves decided to escape from Kentucky using a large sled. They raced over the frozen landscape at full speed until daylight and headed for the house of a man named Kite who had escaped to Ohio before them. Kite took them into his home, then went to get help.

When Kite returned, his house was surrounded by the slave owner and his posse. The fugitives refused to open the door, saying that they were armed and that they would rather die than be returned to slavery. The slave owner and his posse battered down the door and rushed in. After her husband was dragged from the cabin, Margaret, one of the slaves, grabbed a butcher knife from a table and cut the throat of her daughter, saying death was preferable to bringing her up in slavery.

The group was arrested and went to trial. All assured their lawyers that they would "go singing to the gallows" rather than live as slaves again. The unsympathetic court sent the entire group back to slavery. While being transported in a boat, Margaret jumped overboard with another of her children, an infant, in her arms. She was rescued, but the baby drowned.

In the South, slaves were a valuable commodity and were generally resold whenever a slave owner needed money, moved away, or died. The slave trade often led to the breakup of slave families.

19

RELIGIOUS SUPPORT

As George Washington and other slave owners found, there were many northerners who were prepared to help enslaved African-Americans escape to a free state. Most belonged to one of the religious groups that had declared themselves against slavery. The Mennonites in Germantown, Pennsylvania, had declared in 1688 that "There is a saying, that we shall doe to all men like as we will be done ourselves; making no difference of what the generation, descent or colour they are."[9]

Baptist churches formed societies for the gradual abolition of slavery and some Presbyterian congregations urged their members to give their slaves "such good education as to prepare them for a better enjoyment of freedom."[10] In 1842, about 20,000 members of the Methodist church formed an organization to help fugitive slaves. Soon Methodist neighborhoods all over the North were providing "safe houses" for runaways.

One of the most active church groups engaged in helping slaves were the Congregationalists. They organized a colony for escaped slaves and a college in Oberlin, Ohio, which by 1835 became a popular haven for runaways. In fact, a sign that bore the silhouette image of a fugitive running toward the town was set up on a rock near the college, north of the town. A popular tavern also sported a sign depicting a fugitive slave pursued by a tiger, a symbol for slave owners.

Probably the group that did the most work among fugitive slaves were the Quakers, or Society of Friends. As early as 1688, German Quakers living in Germantown, Pennsylvania, had issued a formal protest "against the traffic in the bodies of men and the treatment of men as cattles,"[11] and were eager to help the slaves gain freedom.

The Quakers' opposition to slavery was based on the Bible. They believed that all human souls were equal and they believed in the dignity of people. Socially, they believed that owning slaves resulted in idleness, pride, and vanity since slavery allowed someone else to do the work for others. Economically, they believed slavery prevented the immigrants from other countries from getting jobs because the slaves represented free labor. The Quakers argued that this interfered with the prosperity of those already living in the United States. To those who argued that slave labor was necessary, the Quakers told them, "Poverty does not make Robbery lawful."[12]

Some Quakers did own slaves, but the church urged that they:

> bring up their negroes to some Learning, Reading, and Writing, and endeavor to the utmost of their power in the sweet Love of Truth to instruct and teach 'em the principles of truth and righteousness, and learn them some honest Trade or Imployment, and then set them free.... [13]

In the late 1700s, a committee was formed to visit those Quakers who kept slaves and persuade them nicely to set their slaves free. If that didn't work, church members testified against them in open meetings, then partially excluded them from the society, and finally disowned them completely. At one monthly meeting, thirteen persons were disowned and some who had sold their slaves were ordered to redeem them and set them free. By 1778, under this form of "friendly persuasion," most of the Quaker-owned slaves had been manumitted (freed); by 1782, all were free.

After that, many of the Quakers dedicated their lives to helping the remaining slaves gain freedom. Because they believed that no man should be owned by another, they also believed that the fugitive slave laws were unjust and should not be enforced. They set in operation a method of peacefully disobeying these laws and helping the slaves in any way they could. This operation would one day be known as the Underground Railroad.

TWO
LAYING THE TRACKS
TO FREEDOM

Then lift that manly right hand, bold
ploughman of the wave,
Its branded palm shall prophesy,
"Salvation to the Slave."
— John Greenleaf Whittier[1]

Eventually, a number of events took place which would make the work of aiding slaves even more important. In 1807, a law was passed that prohibited importing slaves from Africa and the Caribbean. If no more slaves could be brought into the country, the value of slaves already owned and those born in the United States increased. Suddenly it was vitally important to slave owners that their slaves be prevented from escaping because they now could not be replaced.

Improvements in agricultural technology also increased the value of slaves. One of the most important was the cotton gin, invented by Eli Whitney in 1793. The machine greatly speeded up the process of cleaning raw cotton, and more and more southern land was devoted to the crop to meet the increased demand. More slaves than ever were needed, and their owners were very vigilant to make sure their slaves did not escape. When slaves did escape, owners doubled their efforts to get them back.

ABOLITION SOCIETIES FORMED

Another threat to slave owners was the growing efficiency of the abolitionists, those seeking the elimination of slavery from American society. At first, these individuals worked on their own throughout the northern states. Then they began to organize and become more powerful.

22

The first abolitionist society was organized in Pennsylvania on April 14, 1775. This was before America was independent. The manumission of a large number of slaves by the Quakers and other abolitionists attracted kidnappers who wanted to sell the freed blacks to slave owners as ex-slaves. The Abolition Society's goal was to make sure this did not happen.

The Abolition Society worked at saving free blacks until the Revolutionary War when it was suspended for a short time. In 1784, it was renewed and in 1787, it changed its name to The Pennsylvania Society for Promoting the Abolition of Slavery, the Relief of Free Negroes unlawfully held in Bondage, and for Improving the Condition of the African Race. Benjamin Franklin was its first president.

The aims of the new society were to:

- educate the public with speeches, essays, and pamphlets
- petition the courts for more favorable laws
- urge and aid the blacks to become self-supporting and useful to the community

Other free states followed Pennsylvania's model, and soon abolitionist societies were founded in many northern areas.

The renewed efforts of slave owners to hold on to their property should have discouraged the abolitionists from interfering, but it didn't. In fact, it seemed to make them more determined than ever to help free the slaves. The abolitionists continued helping those slaves who crossed their paths on the way to safety, and also kept trying to find a peaceable solution to the problem of slavery.

ALTERNATIVES TO SLAVERY

At first, the abolitionists suggested working out a system similar to one used in the West Indies. There, slaves were

Members of an antislavery society listen
to a speaker deplore the evils of slavery
during a convention held in 1840.

allowed to work one day a week in exchange for wages. They could then eventually save up enough money to "buy" their freedom.

Another idea for the peaceful abolition of slavery was to sell the slaves to planters in the West Indies. Still others thought the answer was to colonize the freed blacks someplace west of the Alleghenies or in the new territory of Louisiana. Other ideas were suggested. In 1787, a colony for freed Negroes to be established in Sierra Leone, Africa, was proposed. On December 16, 1826, the Centerville Abolition Society in Pennsylvania proposed to set off a district in the southern part of its territory "for such persons of color as are opposed to emigrating to Hayti [Haiti] or Liberia."[2] But, since none of these proved acceptable to everybody, none was ever carried out.

The main reason for owning slaves was to make money. One peaceful solution, some abolitionists reasoned, lay in hurting the plantation owners economically. These abolitionists suggested boycotting plantation products.

A boycott of plantation sugarcane was planned. It was thought that such a boycott might encourage the slave owners to free their slaves. Abolitionists vowed to use only sugar from maple trees growing in the North. Benjamin Rush, a famous antislavery doctor, said, "I cannot help contemplating a sugar-maple tree with a species of affection and even veneration for I have persuaded myself to behold in it the happy means of rendering the commerce and slavery of our African brethren in the sugar islands as unnecessary, as it has always been inhuman and unjust."[3]

It was estimated that if northerners planted 263,000 sugar-maple trees in New York and Pennsylvania, sugar produced by slaves would eventually be replaced. Although orchards of maple trees were planted, the plan backfired when the cotton gin was invented and cotton became more important than sugar.

THE UNDERGROUND RAILROAD IS BORN

Eventually, then, the antislavery groups' main goal was to hurt the slave owners economically by helping their slaves escape to free states. At first, these efforts were fragmented. As years passed, however, the people helping the slaves became more aware of each other and a kind of nameless, secret organization was formed.

Then, in 1831, a Kentucky slave named Tice Davids escaped to Ohio. When Tice came to the Ohio River, he had no choice but to swim across. His master, not far behind, was determined to capture him. The slave owner found a small boat, called a skiff, and trailed the black fugitive, keeping his bobbing head in sight. He saw Tice wade ashore. The next time he looked, however, the slave had disappeared.

The slave owner put his skiff ashore at the exact spot where Tice had waded out of the river. He spent hours searching for his property, asking everyone he met if they had seen a black man. No one had. Furious, he had to return to Kentucky alone. The slave, he told his disbelieving friends, "...must have gone off on an underground road."[4]

Eight years later a Washington, D.C., reporter, telling of the torture of a captured slave, said he told of a "railroad that went underground all the way to Boston!"[5] After that, the term Underground Railroad was used to describe this loosely knit organization whose aim was to help escaping slaves to safety.

THE FUGITIVE SLAVE LAW OF 1850

In 1850, a new and tougher fugitive slave law was passed. It specified that:

* identification of a fugitive could be made simply on the word of a slave catcher without an effort to find out if it were true or not

- the fugitive could offer no defense
- there would be no trial by jury
- the fee for the commissioner who settled the case would be ten dollars if he found for the master, only five if he freed the slave
- if a federal agent hampered the seizure of the slave, he could be fined a thousand dollars; if any fugitive escaped, whether it was the agent's fault or not, the agent was held responsible for the value of the slave
- persons other than agents could also be fined a thousand dollars and imprisoned for six months if they helped a slave escape.

The new law struck terror in the hearts of many slaves. Those still in bondage felt freedom was forever out of reach. Those who had escaped from the South to the North now feared that their masters would reappear and spirit them away. Even those who had been born free in the North knew that they, too, might be taken and sold in the South just on the word of another person. They believed that a black man with a college degree was suddenly in as much danger as a slave being transported along the Underground Railroad.

And they were right. In fact, these fears were realized at the very hour the bill became law. A free African-American named James Hamlet was seized in New York after a woman visiting from Baltimore swore he was her escaped slave. He was tried within the hour, handcuffed, and transported to Baltimore. But antislavery people were not going to stand idly by. Fifteen hundred people met at the Zion Church that night and raised $500 to buy him back—a process that was legal at that time.

In another incident, an eighteen-year-old black girl escaped to Boston, married a free man, and had two sons. Because she was a former slave, the children were by law considered to be slaves even though their father was free. When the Fugitive Slave Law was passed, therefore, the slave hunters were suddenly interested in this prize—a mother and two male children.

The woman was terrified. Her husband, a seaman, was away at sea. She was so frightened, she dared not leave the house. Days passed and when the family ran out of food, she was forced to go out. She was spotted by a man from her master's plantation. She ran home, got the children, and raced to the home of a friend who in turn took her to a pastor known to help blacks. The pastor spirited her and the children to a steamer sailing for Halifax, Nova Scotia. When her husband returned home months later, he found an empty house. His wife and children had become exiles because of a new law.

UNCLE TOM'S CABIN

When people heard these heartbreaking stories, they were horrified and the ranks of the Underground Railroad swelled. Then, in 1852, a book was published that had an even greater effect on the organization. A woman named Harriet Beecher Stowe had had a child who died of cholera. She later said she felt at her child's grave that she understood how a black mother felt being separated from her child and vowed she would do something special in behalf of the African-Americans.

The result of that vow was a book called *Uncle Tom's Cabin, or Life Among the Lowly.* It was published as a serial

Harriet Beecher Stowe (1811–1896) was an ardent abolitionist. Her book *(inset)* transformed the issue of slavery into a moral battleground and hardened the North's resolve to fight the institution that had become entrenched in the South.

PRICE $1.00 FOR TWO VOLS. — VOL. II.

UNCLE TOM'S CABIN;

OR,

LIFE AMONG THE LOWLY.

BY

HARRIET BEECHER STOWE.

BOSTON:
PUBLISHED BY JOHN P. JEWETT & CO.
CLEVELAND, OHIO:
JEWETT, PROCTOR & WORTHINGTON.
1852.

in 1851 to 1852 in the *National Era,* a Washington, D.C., antislavery newspaper, and in book form in 1852. Within one year, it sold 300,000 copies. The woman who described herself in a letter as "a little bit of a woman— somewhat more than forty, about as thin and dry as a pinch of snuff: never very much to look at on my best days, and looking like a used-up article now"[6] suddenly became very famous and very rich.

Harriet, who had been raised in Cincinnati and Boston and knew very little about slavery except what she had seen on her visits to the South, described her book as "...a collection and arrangement of real incidents—of actions really performed, of words and expressions really uttered."[7] Though she felt bound to put these incidents, words, and expressions on paper, she felt that few people would want to read them. She wrote that she worried "nobody would hear, nobody would read, nobody would pity; that this frightful system, which had already pursued its victims into the free States, might at last even threaten them in Canada."[8]

Harriet set her story in Kentucky: To pay his debts, plantation owner Arthur Shelby has to sell his faithful black slave, Tom, and a child Harry, who is the son of Eliza, another slave. When Eliza hears Harry is to be sold, she embarks on a desperate flight across the frozen Ohio River where she is rescued by Quakers with the Underground Railroad. Meanwhile, little Eva, the daughter of a wealthy Louisiana planter, is saved from drowning by Tom. Out of gratitude, the planter, Augustine St. Clare, buys Tom and gives him the duties of a household servant. Unfortunately, St. Clare dies and Tom is sold to the brutal owner of the Red River plantation, Simon Legree. Shelby sets out to save his old servant, but is too late.

FLIGHT TO CANADA

While readers were weeping over the fate of Uncle Tom and Eliza, a large number of blacks, panic-stricken because of the new fugitive slave law, were leaving the United States for Canada. Forty blacks left Massachusetts for Canada within thirty-five hours after the bill became law. Some 500 out of 942 blacks left Columbia, Pennsylvania, and a settlement in Sandy Lake, Pennsylvania, disappeared completely. At a small town in New York, an entire church of eighty-two members, including the pastor, mysteriously disappeared overnight. A Baptist church in Rochester lost 114 of its 141 members. It was estimated that at least 6,000 fugitives fled their homes, a number that one person noted, was "larger...than that of escaping Puritans who had come to America in the 1600s."[9]

These events brought the plight of the slaves to the public's attention, and suddenly the Underground Railroad was swamped with requests for help from both northern and southern African-Americans anxious to flee to Canada. The Underground Railroad was also swamped with new volunteers who, inspired by *Uncle Tom's Cabin* and infuriated by the Fugitive Slave Law of 1850, wanted to help. Practically overnight there was more money, more supplies, and more respectability. The people on the Underground Railroad would soon be laying the tracks to freedom in great numbers.

THREE
WORKING ON THE RAILROAD

*I heard the wail of the captive. I felt his pang
of distress, and the iron entered my soul.
—Benjamin Lundy, 1815, Publisher of*
The Genius of Universal Emancipation,
an antislavery newspaper[1]

As the tracks were being laid across the United States
for the railroad, the people working on the Underground Railroad used railroad titles to describe their
members. They referred to themselves and each other as
"brakemen," "firemen," "agents," "station masters," and
"conductors." Sometimes, within a bigger town or city
there might be a "manager" or "superintendent." There
were even "presidents" of the railroad in some areas.
There were no dues in this organization, but anyone
wishing to contribute money could become a "stock-
holder."

Slowly but surely, as the Underground Railroad
"tracks" were laid across the North, railroad terms were
also applied to the safe places for hiding. The houses
where the slaves were hidden were called "depots" and
"stations." To move to the next house of safety was "to
catch the next train."

WHITE CONDUCTORS AND STATION MASTERS

Once the "tracks" were laid, people from all walks of life
came to get on board the Underground Railroad. Young
and old, black and white, they eagerly volunteered their
services. Some held high positions in state and federal

government; others were ordinary folks, like the tailor in Philadelphia who spent his days sitting at his window sewing, watching the road for a fugitive so he could run out and save him.

Some Underground Railroad workers were more enthusiastic than others. Not for them the slow, cautious, secret ways of the peaceful Quakers. They wanted things done quickly, even if it meant bloodshed. There were traveling preachers, for instance, who wandered through the South, encouraging slaves to arm themselves with weapons and to kill, if necessary, in order to gain their freedom.

JOHN FAIRFIELD

Oddly enough, one of the most enthusiastic white workers to use violent means of freeing the slaves was a southerner, John Fairfield, a Virginian, who grew up in a family of slaveholders. As a young man, he decided to help one of his uncle's slaves escape on a trip to Ohio. He and the slave had played together as boys and grew up together. John managed to get his friend Bill to safety. Before his Underground career was over, it is said he helped several thousand slaves escape.

Fairfield was described by Levi Coffin, his Underground Railroad contact, as "a wicked man, daring and reckless in his actions yet faithful to the trust reposed in him, and benevolent to the poor."[2] Those who knew him said he had no fear, but, unlike the Quakers, he traveled heavily armed. He escaped several times from jail and each time he escaped, he vowed he would liberate a slave for every day he had spent in prison.

Fairfield, because of his violent nature, was often in danger. He once showed Levi Coffin several bullet holes in his clothes, a flesh wound on one arm, and a flesh wound on the arm of one of the fugitives he had brought out. Coffin, a Quaker, often chastised him for using violence and urged him to love his enemies:

33

Love the devil! Fairfield exclaimed. Slave-holders are all devils and it is no harm to kill the devil. I do not intend to hurt people if they keep out of the way, but if they slip in between me and liberty, they must take the consequences. When I undertake to conduct slaves out of bondage I feel that it is my duty to defend them, even to the last drop of my blood. [3]

Fairfield was often described as being as ragged and dirty as some of the fugitives he rescued. This, and perhaps a good dose of fear, made them respect and obey him. One of the fugitives he rescued recalled,

I never saw such a man as Fairfield. He told us he would take us out of slavery or die in the attempt, if we would do our part, which we promised to do. We all agreed to fight till we died, rather than be captured. Fairfield said he wanted no cowards in the company; if we were attacked and one of us showed cowardice or started to run, he would shoot him down. [4]

Fairfield would wear many disguises whenever he traveled into the South to bring the slaves out. One time he would be a salesman dealing in chicken and eggs; another time he would pose as a slave trader. His most elaborate scheme found him posing as a salt trader near Charleston, Virginia. Several blacks in Ohio had relatives in slavery at or near the salt works there and they begged Fairfield to bring them out. He went to the salt works and with his helpers, all black, began contacting the slaves he had come to save. Some of these slaves were good boatmen, as were Fairfield's men. It was decided they would pretend to build boats for the salt trade, then use them to escape.

When the first boat was finished, one of the escaping slaves boarded it with one of Fairfield's men on a Saturday night. They silently glided down the river a short distance to a spot where they pulled over to the shore and took on a group of slaves. When the loss of the boat was discovered on Monday morning, Fairfield pretended to be furious. He vowed to put a strict watch on the second boat but that, too, disappeared the following Saturday, along with ten or twelve more slaves. Fairfield took off in pursuit with a posse made up of local men. Once across the river, he suggested that they split up and he would meet them at a certain point. Of course, he was never seen again.

About 1861, Fairfield eventually opened a small store in a black settlement in Indiana, but two years later he disappeared forever. Levi Coffin often thought he had been killed in Tennessee because he heard there was an insurrection among the slaves there. Several were killed and some were hanged when they were captured. It was said that the leader of the group was a white man who was also killed. No one will ever know for sure whether that white man was John Fairfield.

JOHN BROWN

Another man who had a plan for increasing the work of the Underground Railroad by using force was a white Connecticut man named John Brown. Brown wandered from job to job, plagued by ill fortune before he became interested in the slavery issue in 1850. His father, Owen Brown, had been one of the first men to harbor slaves in eastern Ohio. The son followed by opening his house to fugitives.

John Brown began to consider slavery as a state of war. He devised a plan to pick out twenty-five slaves who were above average in physical and mental capabilities. He would supply them with arms and ammunition and organize them into an army of squads of five on a line of 25 miles (40.2 km). They would go down into the fields and try to induce other slaves to join them.

JERMAIN LOGUEN

LUCRETIA MOTT

FREDERICK DOUGLASS

ALLAN PINKERTON

JOSIAH HENSON

THOMAS GARRETT

WILLIAM L. GARRISON

SUSAN B. ANTHONY

JONATHAN WALKER

Agents of the Underground Railroad

Thousands of people – including former slaves, freeborn blacks, white reformers, and clergy members – worked to open and safeguard the passage of slaves to freedom. Starting at top row, from left to right:

Jermain Loguen (c. 1813–1872). A fugitive slave, Underground agent, and ordained minister who helped 1,500 escapees and founded several black schools in New York State.

Lucretia Coffin Mott (1793–1880). A Quaker advocate for abolition and women's rights.

Frederick Douglass (c. 1817–1895). A fugitive slave and fiery abolitionist speaker, whose print shop in Rochester, New York, served as a depot for the Underground

John Greenleaf Whittier (1807–1892). A Quaker poet and a powerful voice for the abolitionist movement.

Allan Pinkerton (1819–1884). Founder of the famous detective agency that still bears his name, he operated an Underground depot at his cooper's shop near Chicago.

Josiah Henson (1789–1883). A slave who escaped to Canada and traveled as an abolitionist and businessman.

Thomas Garrett (1789–1871). A businessman who reputedly aided more than 2,700 slaves to freedom.

Mary Ann Shadd (1823–1893). Daughter of a black Underground agent, the Quaker-educated teacher, writer, and editor urged blacks to permanently emigrate from the States.

William Lloyd Garrison (1805–1879). Journalist and publisher of the famous antislavery journal *The Liberator.*

Susan B. Anthony (1820–1906). Daughter of a Quaker, she was a teacher who spoke out for abolition and spearheaded the fight for women's suffrage.

Jonathan Walker (1799–1878). Imprisoned for helping seven slaves on an attempted escape to the Bahamas, Walker was branded on the hand with the letters "SS" for "Slave Stealer."

William Still (1821–1902. An industrious worker in the Philadelphia Underground, who kept rare day-to-day records of the organization's operations.

John Brown hoped eventually to raise an army of a hundred blacks. He would drill and train them to rescue slaves in large numbers. Out of those he rescued, Brown would keep those who were brave and strong; those he considered weak and cowardly would be sent or led by him north on the Underground Railroad.

Brown spent most of his time visiting Underground Railroad workers, trying to win their support. In the winter of 1857–58, he visited St. Catherines, a town in Canada, where the famous black Underground worker Harriet Tubman took her fugitives. Harriet was amazed when she met with Brown in a forest near St. Catherines. She had been having recurring dreams in which the head of a snake appeared on rocks, then turned into the head of an old man with a long white beard and glittering eyes. (Brown had glittering eyes and a long white beard.) In her dream, the man would look as if he wanted to say something to her, then a crowd of men would swarm in and strike down his head. Harriet realized when she saw Brown for the first time that he was that old man.

Brown told Harriet he needed to know the routes she had used and the names of possible recruits for his army. He wanted her to help him lead the slaves to Canada. Although Harriet hated bloodshed, she said she would help him.

Despite their meeting and plans, Harriet was never able to help John Brown. Brown had chosen the United States government arsenal at Harpers Ferry, Virginia, for his first attack and on October 16, 1859, he and his band of rebels seized the town. Federal troops under Robert E. Lee were sent in and ten of Brown's "army" died. John Brown was wounded, arrested, and charged with treason. He was hanged on December 2, 1859.

LAURA HAVILAND

Most Underground Railroad conductors, however, were more peaceful and did not approve of the violent ways of John Brown and John Fairfield. They were more like Laura Haviland, the petite, prim Quaker from Michigan who spent her energies raising money to found the Raisin Institute, a school for both white and black children.

Laura Haviland's Underground activities consisted of helping slaves whenever the opportunity arose. In 1847, for example, she set out to find the family of John White, an escaped slave who worked as a farmhand near the Raisin Institute. Disguised as a berry picker, Laura went into Kentucky to find John's wife. Her plan was to inform Mrs. White of her husband's whereabouts and to help her escape. Unfortunately, Mrs. White never appeared and when John went in later to try to find her himself, he was arrested and thrown into jail. Laura raised the $350 to purchase him.

WILLIAM McKEEVER

Many workers joined the Underground Railroad because they had experienced the inhumanity of slavery firsthand. William McKeever, for instance, saw slaves for the first time as a child in 1830. They were chained together and a slave driver was flogging and cursing them as they made their way down the street. McKeever's father shouted at the slave drivers, but they paid no attention to him at first. He followed them out of the village shouting Bible quotations and insults.

Finally, one of the slave drivers turned on him and suggested it might be safer for the old man if he returned to town. McKeever watched as his father tore open his shirt and dared them to shoot him through the heart. "This is the only thing that will stop me," he shouted. [5] The slave drivers ignored him and went their way, but this scene had a lasting effect on young William. He went on to become one of the most active Underground Railroad workers in Pennsylvania.

39

LEVI COFFIN

Levi Coffin, who was born in North Carolina in 1789, also learned about slavery firsthand at a very young age. One day when he was only seven, he was watching his father chop wood. A group of black men approached. They were handcuffed and chained together. Behind them was a man on horseback who hurried them along by snapping a long whip over their backs. As they passed, Levi's father asked one of the black men, "Why do they chain you?" The black man said, "They have taken us away from our wives and children, and they chain us lest we should make our escape and go back to them."[6]

Levi wondered how it would feel if his own father were taken away and chained. He never forgot the incident. Another time he accompanied his father on a trip to a fishery owned by two brothers named Crump, who were slave owners. The Crumps sometimes allowed their slaves to fish at night and sell the fish to visitors. One of the slaves was talking to Levi's father after selling him some fish. As the two sat around the breakfast fire, a young nephew of the Crumps approached the group. He seemed furious that the slave would be seen talking to white people. He seized a stick from the fire and struck the slave across the head, baring his skull, covering him with blood. As Mr. Coffin protested and tried to help the slave, Levi fled, his breakfast forgotten, to cry in the nearby woods.

As incident after incident was etched on his mind, it was natural that Levi Coffin would begin helping slaves at an early age. His first Underground experience occurred when he was fifteen years old and still living in North Carolina. It was the custom there to make a "frolic" of any of the annual chores such as cornhusking or log-rolling. The neighbors and their slaves all pitched in and when the work was finished, they celebrated.

Levi was at just such a frolic when he struck up a

conversation with one of the slaves being taken farther south by a slave dealer. He learned that the slave, Stephen, was freeborn but had been kidnapped from a "negro house" (a house where blacks were sheltered) in Baltimore. He was gagged, bound, and driven to Virginia where he had been sold to his present slave dealer.

Levi told his father and together they sat about contacting Edward Lloyd, a Quaker, to whom Stephen had been apprenticed before his kidnapping. Lloyd's brother, Hugh, and two other Quakers arrived two days later and reclaimed Stephen. They took him to Georgia where they initiated a lawsuit to prove he was being illegally held. Six months later, Stephen was free.

That was the start of a very busy Underground career for Levi Coffin. Before that career was over, he would be called the President of the Underground Railroad. Coffin said that title came about when he helped seventeen slaves successfully escape. As the slave catchers, defeated, passed his plain, square home several weeks later, they supposedly said, "There's an Underground Railroad around here and Levi Coffin is its president."[7] This quote was repeated so often and Levi became so well known that letters were addressed to "Levi Coffin, President of the Underground Railroad."

RUNAWAY SLAVES WHO JOINED THE UNDERGROUND RAILROAD

Many fugitives who obtained their freedom went on to become Underground Railroad workers themselves, working alongside the very people who had helped them gain their freedom.

John Mason, an escaped slave from Kentucky, risked his newfound freedom by going to work on the Underground Railroad. He slipped back into Kentucky and during a nineteen-month period led 265 slaves to freedom. Eventually he was captured (both of his arms were broken when he resisted), and he was sold and taken to New Orleans.

Ermene Cain, a black janitor in the courthouse of Washington County, Pennsylvania, for forty-five years, was an Underground Railroad worker. Samuel W. Dorsey, "a colored barber" in Washington, Pennsylvania, was an Underground Railroad worker. In Wheeling, West Virginia, "Old Naylor" or "Free" Naylor (so called because he was old and free), devoted his life to helping slaves to freedom. He was so respected that after the Civil War when he moved to West Middletown, Pennsylvania, and was very poor, neighbors donated land, labor, and lumber and built him a house where he spent the remainder of his days.

Another of the blacks who escaped from slavery and went on to help countless other fugitives was William Still. His father, Levin, had purchased his own freedom. His mother, Sidney, had led her children to freedom, using the North Star as a guide. Their youngest son, William, eventually became executive secretary of the Philadelphia Anti-Slavery Society. As secretary, he kept meticulous records of fugitives the society aided through the Underground Railroad. In 1872, he wrote *The Underground Railroad*, which became one of the most important books on the subject.

Josiah Henson was one of the famous slaves who returned the kindness of the Underground Railroad by becoming a member. He had originally escaped from his master by wandering through the wildernesses of Indiana and Ohio and was chased by wolves and nearing starvation when he was found by Indians. He was eventually led to Canada by Underground Railroad workers.

Henson, refusing to rest once he had reached safety, became very active in helping his fellow escapees. He led a movement to have blacks buy their own land. When he realized that tobacco could probably be raised quite easily in the new land, he convinced slaves to raise the crop since they already knew so much about it. He started a community called the Dawn Settlement, a manual-labor school, and a sawmill which produced choice black walnut wood for pianos. In between, he went back into slave territory many times to bring other slaves to freedom. When he went to exhibit his wood at the World's Fair in London in 1852, Henson became the first ex-slave to be granted an audience with Queen Victoria. He also met with the archibishop of Canterbury to tell him of his adventures in bringing hundreds of slaves to safety.

FREDERICK DOUGLASS

Although many of the exploits of the conductors were kept secret, sometimes workers stood out for their dramatic personalities. Such was the case with two other black workers, Frederick Douglass and Harriet Tubman. Born a slave, Frederick Douglass had seen his family and friends brutally treated by their owners. Frederick persuaded his Baltimore owner to allow him to "hire his time." This was a common practice in southern cities. The slave was hired out to work for others. The owner kept most of the money the slave received; the slave got to keep a small sum for incidentals he might want to buy.

But Frederick did not spend his money on "incidentals." He hoarded his money until he had enough to escape. Then he borrowed the free papers, which were legal documents verifying that the holder was a free person, from a free friend (who knew that without those valuable papers he himself could be kidnapped and sold into slavery). Frederick made his way to New Bedford, Massachusetts, were he eventually became a renowned, eloquent speaker and effective recruiter for the Underground Railroad. He later said, "I could take not a step in it without exposing myself to fine and imprisonment, ...but in face of this fact, I can say, I never did more congenial, attractive, fascinating, and satisfactory work."[8]

UNITED STATES OF AMERICA,

STATE OF ILLINOIS,
Madison County, } ss. } To all to whom these Presents may come—GREETING:

Know Ye, That *John Tony*
a person of Color, about *twenty seven* years of age, *post five*
feet *six* inches high, *Mulatto*
complexion,

has exhibited, presented and filed, in the Office of the Clerk of the Circuit
Court of the County and State aforesaid, a **CERTIFICATE,** duly authen-
ticated, of **FREEDOM,** as such person of Color, *has a scar*
over the left Eye Brow a scratch across the cheek born a
scar on the left hand from Tayler to Mark

Now, therefore, I, **WM. TYLER BROWN,** *Clerk* of the Circuit
Court of Madison County, State of Illinois, **CERTIFY,** That said
John Tony is a FREE PERSON OF COLOR, a resi-
dent or citizen of the State of Illinois, and entitled to be respected accord-
ingly, in Person and Property, at all times and places, in the due prosecu-
tion of *his* Lawful concerns.

In Testimony whereof, I have, to these Presents,
signed my name, and affixed the Seal of
said Court, at Edwardsville, this 2 8th
day of *November* in the year of our
Lord one thousand eight hundred and *forty-four*

Wm T. Brown Clerk.

HARRIET TUBMAN

Probably the most famous African-American Underground worker of the entire period was Harriet Tubman. Harriet, born in Maryland, had watched her two older sisters sold and taken away. She was hired out to a white woman who beat her, then to a man who overworked her in the fields. It was during this time that Harriet began to show the spirit that would eventually transform her into an excellent Underground Railroad worker.

Harriet once blocked the doorway of a slave hut to keep an overseer from hitting another slave with a 2-pound (.91-kg) brass weight. When the overseer lashed out, Harriet received the brunt of the blow. For the rest of her life, she often fell into a sudden, deep sleep or swoon.

When Harriet's master died, all his slaves were to be sold, as often was the case. Harriet went to the home of a white woman who had promised to help her if she ever needed it. The woman handed her a slip of paper with two names on it—places where it would be safe to stop on a trip north.

Harriet convinced her two brothers to escape with her. They started out, but the brothers turned back. She continued alone, hiding in underbrush along the road whenever she heard hoofbeats coming. After all, she would be easy to spot because of the deep scar on her forehead from the brass weight blow and the scars on the back of her neck from having been beaten.

Harriet's first stop was at a farm, and it was here that she first saw how the Underground Railroad operated. The woman who answered her knock handed her a

The free papers of one John Jones were used as legal proof that the bearer was a free person.

broom to sweep the yard so it would look like she belonged there. That night, the farmer put Harriet in a wagon filled with produce, threw blankets over her, and started off down the road. At daybreak the wagon stopped and the farmer told Harriet where the next stop was.

Harriet arrived in Pennsylvania after traveling 90 miles (145 km), sleeping on the ground, being rowed up and down rivers by strangers, concealed in a haycock, spending a week hidden in a potato hole in a cabin and in the attic of a Quaker home. When she crossed into Pennsylvania, she later said, "I looked at my hands to see if I was the same person now I was free. There was such a glory over everything, the sun came like gold through the trees, and over the fields, and I felt like I was in heaven."[9]

After she settled in Philadelphia, Harriet worked steadily, night and day, at menial jobs and saved every cent she could so she could rescue her relatives still left in the South. She also visited the Philadelphia Vigilante Committee headquarters in her spare time and got to know J. Miller McKim, the president, and William Still, the secretary of the committee.

It was at the committee headquarters that she first heard that her sister, her sister's husband, John, and their two children were going to try to escape. The Underground Railroad had made plans to get them as far as Baltimore, but they needed someone to get them to Philadelphia. Harriet volunteered and her career began.

Like many Underground Railroad workers, Harriet learned she had to be daring, cunning, and brave if she wanted to bring her charges out safely. If she felt one person was endangering the group, she was not beyond pulling out a pistol and barking orders in her heavy rolling voice. "Dead niggers tell no tales," she would tell the culprits. "You go on or die." When she was taking a slave, Joe Bailey, his brother, and two other slaves to safety, they balked at wading across the icy water of a river they had come to. Peter said, "I'll wade no freezin' water for no crazy woman." Harriet turned on them and said, "You try to go back, try to run back to the woods, and you'll never run any more. You go on with me or you die."[10] Then she waded across the river herself, holding her gun high over her head. The others hesitated, then plunged into the freezing water.

Harriet's physical disability—the result of her early head wound—was the one thing that worried her on her trips into the South. She was terrified that she might fall asleep in the middle of an escape, and she sometimes did. On the trip with Joe Bailey, they were walking along the road instead of in the woods because it was faster. Suddenly the scar from the old head wound began to throb and she fell asleep. When she awoke, she was horrified to find her puzzled charges standing in plain sight by the roadside, wondering what to do with their sleeping guide.

Despite her disability, Harriet became one of the most famous of the Underground Railroad conductors. William Still once said:

Her success was wonderful. Time and again she made successful visits to Maryland on the Underground Rail Road, and would be absent for weeks at a time, running daily risks while making preparations for herself and passengers. Great fears were entertained for her safety, but she seemed wholly devoid of personal fear. The idea of being captured by slave-hunters or slave-holders, seemed never to enter her mind.[11]

Harriet became known as General Tubman or "Moses" and was described by William Still as a "woman of no pretensions, indeed, a more ordinary specimen of humanity could hardly be found among the most unfortunate-looking farm hands of the South...."[12]

47

Tubman *(far left)*, in a rare photograph taken
with some of the slaves she helped to free

It was estimated that Harriet Tubman led some 300 slaves to safety during her time with the Underground Railroad. At one time, rewards of up to $40,000 were offered for her capture, dead or alive. Despite the rewards, she was never captured. On a tablet at the front entrance of the courthouse in Auburn, New York, where she died on March 10, 1913, are the words she used to describe her success: "On my Underground Railroad I nebber run my train off de track an' I nebber los' a passenger."[13]

Instead of simply delivering her charges to the first Underground Railroad house in the North, Harriet insisted on seeing her charges all the way to Canada. On one trip, she was accompanying a runaway on the train. All the way to Niagara Falls, he sat with his head on his hand, refusing to look at his surroundings, sure he would be captured and returned to slavery at any moment. Finally, halfway across the bridge between New York and Canada, Harriet nudged him.

"You done shook the lion's paw," she told him, meaning he was free from slavery.

The man sprang to his feet, suddenly animated. He shouted, "Oh, go and carry the news! One more soul got safe!"[14]

This was what Harriet and the Underground Railroad workers lived for.

FOUR
THE HARDSHIPS OF RAILROAD WORK

*I have got some nice books (old ones) coming across
the water. But, alas me! such is the state of poor
fugitive slaves, that I must attend to living men,
and not to dead books, and all this winter my time
has been occupied with these poor souls.*
—Theodore Parker, Boston theologian[1]

Not everyone agreed with the philosophies of the Underground Railroad. A number of books and newspaper articles appeared criticizing the organization. In 1853, for instance, a novel called *Mr. Frank, the Underground Rail-Agent* was written by an anonymous author. It ridiculed the Underground Railroad, the Quakers, and pro-slavery politicians. Another book, *Abolition Unveiled*, published in 1857, accused the Underground Railroad of enticing slaves away. And *Disclosures and Confessions of Franklin A. Wilmot, with an accurate Account of the Under-Ground Railroad*, written in 1860, accused the organization of political prejudice.

Newspapers were particularly critical of the Underground Railroad. The editor of the *Syracuse Courier* complained, "The so-called 'Agent' of the Underground Railroad not only stalks through our streets in open noonday, but publicly drives along his wagonloads of deluded 'fugitives,' boastingly appropriates the funds placed at his disposal to pay their way to Canada."[2] The *Cincinnati Daily Enquirer* called the Underground Railroad workers "fanatics of the Western Reserve."[3] In 1850, the *New York Herald* published an article entitled "Practical Operations of the Underground Railroad," which said the

50

fugitives were destitute and miserable and Underground Railroad agents were selling the slaves and pocketing the money.

Some critics even blamed the sale of slaves on the Underground Railroad. In 1856, a Delaware newspaper reported the sale of fifteen slaves and blamed the sale on the fact that the slave owner learned the slaves were trying to escape and would probably do so with the help of the Underground Railroad. A St. Louis reporter said the Underground Railroad was "driving heretofore kind masters to risk the future comfort of their negroes by selling them to strangers."[4] Another reporter wrote that ". . . for every slave the Abolitionists have successfully run to Canada, thousands who remained behind have felt their bonds heavier."[5]

Critics also attacked the way money was spent on the Underground Railroad. Some did not like American funds being funneled to Canada. Some complained that because the society was so secret, no one was accountable for the money they were given. Many thought the money should be spent on abolishing slavery, not helping those slaves who managed to escape. Maria W. Chapman, a member of the Anti-Slavery Society, said the money was being used to "shelter two-and-a-half thousand, instead of freeing two-and-a-half millions." She argued that to work on the Underground Railroad was to "hide from tyranny, instead of defying it."[6]

Such criticism made life difficult for the Underground Railroad workers. They were ridiculed in political cartoons, became the butt of fantastically untrue stories, or were the object of jokes, insults, and rude gestures. Neighbors spied on them. Slave owners, and slave catchers watched their houses for signs of runaways. Their children were sometimes shunned in school; the workers were hissed at when they tried to talk at town meetings. They might be avoided in church or even asked to withdraw from church membership.

Some opponents of slavery were forced to give up their homes, and some even had to move to another state because of the criticisms and the dangers that resulted. When it was discovered that he was harboring an escaped slave, Levi Coffin's cousin Jesse Stanley had to leave his home in North Carolina and settle in Philadelphia. He did not return home for twenty years.

THE PRICE WAS HIGH

In addition to suffering harassment from neighbors and acquaintances, Underground Railroad workers also suffered financially. As early as the eighteenth century, costly penalties had been imposed for those caught helping fugitive slaves. Maryland levied a fine of 500 pounds of tobacco for lodging a runaway for one night, 1,000 pounds for the second night, and 1,500 pounds for each succeeding night. Citizens of New Netherland who hid or fed a fugitive slave were fined 50 guilders. Anyone helping a runaway slave in Virginia could be fined twenty pounds of tobacco for each night's hospitality.

Far from making money from helping free the slaves, as some newspapers suggested, many Underground Railroad workers faced financial ruin as the courts imposed stiffer fines for disobeying the fugitive slave laws. In 1833, a group of Pennsylvania Quakers were fined $4,000 (a great sum for the time) for obstructing a slave owner who was trying to recover his slave. In 1847, workers in Michigan were fined $2,752 for helping six runaway slaves. Thomas Garrett was fined so heavily he was left penniless. Still he told a judge, "Thee hasn't left me a dollar, but I wish to say to thee and to all in this court room, that if anyone knows of a fugitive who wants a shelter and a friend, send him to Thomas Garrett, and he will befriend him."[7]

Many Underground workers faced financial ruin not only because of the fines imposed but also because of court costs. (Some cases went all the way to the Supreme Court.) These costs could amount to thousands of dollars. In 1848, for example, Daniel Kaufman of Cumberland, Pennsylvania, was tried for sheltering a family of thirteen slaves in his barn and giving them transportation north. Kaufman's trial costs eventually totaled over $4,000. (Fortunately for Kaufman and many other Underground Railroad workers, an organization called the Defensive League of Freedom paid all the costs, fines, and expenses.)

> For Sale: a negro boy who has thirteen years to serve; he is stoute and healthy. Apply at the Office of The Reporter.[8]

Such advertisements as this one found in a Pennsylvania newspaper in 1813 were a fact of life during the 1800s and some Underground Railroad workers spent large sums of their own money to buy slaves in order to free them. Alice Eliza Hamilton wrote, "The feelings of some among us, who scrupulously maintain that no combination of circumstances can justify the purchase of a slave, had been closely tried when called upon to save their fellow human beings from slavery."[9]

Indeed, Alice's beliefs were "closely tried" when an escaped slave who was staying at her house was apprehended and returned to slavery, leaving her husband and baby behind. Alice bought the woman back for $900 and the family was reunited.

Some slaves were sold for prices as low as $70 to $100, a sum that could be raised fairly easily by Underground workers. Other were more costly. Anthony Burns, who was returned from Boston to slavery in Virginia and North Carolina, was later purchased through the efforts of a free African-American, Leonard Frimes, for $1,325. Frederick Douglass was also one of those freed through similar means for $750.

Besides spending large amounts of their own money,

Underground Railroad workers also spent time away from their business and families trying to raise money for their cause. When Levi Coffin needed money for his underground work, his favorite trick was to go to a store and ask the owner if he had any "stock" in the Underground Railroad. If the owner said yes, Levi would tell him he was there to call the assessment on the stock. Levi would then collect a dollar or two and move on to the next merchant until he had enough money for his current project.

Levi also spent a large amount of time organizing speaking tours for ex-fugitives as a means of raising money for the cause. When one financially troubled Georgia slave owner needed to sell his slaves to satisfy his debts, two of the slaves sold were a beautiful woman named Louisa, and her mother. On the day of the sale, the women were sold to different masters. As Louisa was led away, she heard her mother crying and praying. She looked back and saw her mother on her knees in the midst of the crowd, tears streaming down her face.

Louisa never forgot the sight of her mother at the slave sale and so, when she was later freed, she began searching for her mother. When she found her, her mother's master said Louisa could have her for one thousand dollars. Louisa contacted Levi Coffin and he advised her, as he had others, to go to different towns and tell her story to raise money. She did so and managed to get almost all the money she needed to purchase her mother's freedom.

DANGERS OF WORKING ON THE UNDERGROUND RAILROAD

Working on the Underground Railroad was not only time-consuming and financially draining, it was also dangerous. Slave owners had invested large amounts of money in their slaves and they did not like their being taken away. Sometimes they offered huge rewards for the capture of an Underground Railroad worker. For instance, Maryland officials offered $10,000 for the capture of Thomas Garrett. (Garrett responded by writing an open letter to the officials saying he was worth at least $20,000!)

Underground workers also were often threatened, both verbally and in writing. Threats of murder became so frequent that Garrett's black friends took turns guarding him. Levi Coffin also received many threats during his work with the Underground Railroad. He once received anonymous letters warning him that his store, porkhouse, and dwelling would be burned to the ground. One letter from Kentucky said that a body of armed men were on their way to destroy the town on a certain night and warned him to flee or be killed. Levi and his friends refused to be intimidated. As he later wrote:

> . . .On the night appointed [they] retired to their beds as usual and slept peacefully. We placed no sentinels to give warning of danger, and had no extra company at our house to guard our lives. We retired to rest at the usual hour, and were not disturbed during the night. In the morning the buildings were all there— there was no smell of fire, no sign of the terrible destruction threatened. I heard only one person who was alarmed, and he did not live in town. [10]

Unfortunately, the threats and rewards did sometimes lead to violence. Slave owners or their agents forced their way into houses which they believed were harboring slaves. Brickbats and stones were thrown through windows. Posses were formed and slave owners took the law into their own hands.

One Underground worker who found out that aiding escaped slaves could have serious consequences was Isaac

Members of the Executive Committee of the
Pennsylvania Anti-Slavery Society, 1851

Hopper, a Quaker. In 1801, Hopper lived in Philadelphia, which was a crossroads for slaves escaping from Maryland. He was a member of the very active Philadelphia Abolition Society, oversaw a school for black children and taught a school for black parents at night.

Hopper was hard at work helping slaves when he heard about a ten-year-old black boy being spirited out of the city by a Frenchman. It was rumored that the Frenchman, who was traveling down the river on a packet (a kind of sailing ship), was going to take the boy back to France with him to try to sell him there. The child's mother frantically contacted Hopper.

Hopper found a ferryman who could take him out to the packet. He climbed aboard and found the kidnappers in a cabin with half a dozen friends. Fearlessly, Hopper demanded the return of the boy. A struggle began. They tried to throw Hopper overboard, but he clutched desperately to the neckerchief of one of the attackers despite repeated blows to his body and face. Meanwhile, the captain, afraid of being arrested, had lowered the child into the ferryboat. Hopper saw the child and, wresting himself free of his attackers, leapt into the ferryboat in a dramatic escape.

Despite the dangers, Hopper continued his work, so it was inevitable that he would be involved in more dramatic rescues. In another adventure, he approached a group of men who were holding an African-American hostage in a shabby tavern near a wharf. The men threw him out of the window. His fall was broken by a pile of empty casks below. Undaunted, Hopper climbed up on a high wooden fence, lifted himself to the roof of a shed, and sneaked through a window into the room adjoining that of the captive. He threw open the door, rushed in with an open penknife, cut the ropes of the captive and shouted, "Follow me!" Before the astonished guards could move, the two were running down the street.

In New York in the summer of 1834, thirty-one houses and two churches were destroyed by a mob of

In the summer of 1834, angry pro-slavery supporters
staged two days of riots in New York
City, burning and looting buildings.

slavery supporters. They broke into abolitionist Lewis Tappan's home and threw his furniture out of the window. They built a bonfire out of the furniture. Mounted police waded in. The rioters tore down fences and used the fence posts for clubs. They overturned carts and used them for barricades. For two days the battle continued.

Meanwhile, Tappan had armed the clerks in his store with guns. On the third day of the riot, a rock was thrown through the store window. The sound of crashing wood followed and a mob pushed into the store. The clerks stood unmoving behind the counters, their guns pointed at the angry trespassers. Defeated, the mob turned and pushed its way back down the street to sack an African-American church and set fire to the homes of several black people.

Unfortunately, Tappan's worries were not over. Neighbors hanged him in effigy. His business suffered because his old customers were afraid to come into his store. Insurance companies refused to cover him or his property. Banks would not lend him money. One morning he opened his mail, and a slave's ear and a piece of rope fell out. Georgia offered a reward of $12,000 to any man who could bring Tappan across the border; New Orleans added $20,000 to the bounty. It was even rumored that one unnamed state offered $3,000 for his ear as well.

Another Underground worker who became the object of mob violence was William Lloyd Garrison. When the Boston Female Antislavery Society invited him to address their October meeting, a reward of $100 was offered to any man who could bring him to "the tar kettle before dark" (meaning they would tar and feather him and run him out of town). The men of the town were determined to convince the women to attend to domestic matters instead of dabbling in antislavery issues. Thirty women, black and white, defied the men and were on hand when Garrison's speech began. Soon they could hear a mob forming outside. The mayor arrived.

"Ladies, if you do not wish to see a scene of bloodshed and confusion, go home!" he said.

Mrs. Maria Weston Chapman rose and spoke for the group. "If this is the last bailiwick of freedom, we may as well die here as anywhere," she told him.

The mob broke down the door. Garrison escaped through a back window, but the mob discovered him hiding in a carpenter's shop and tried to throw him out of a second-story window. One man talked them out of it, but they tied a rope around Garrison and dragged him into the street. Finally the police came, but Garrison was still in danger. When the police tried to take him to jail, the mob began to untie the horses from the carriage and break down the doors. The police beat them off and galloped away with their quarry. Finally, safe in prison, Garrison wrote on the cell wall: "William Lloyd Garrison put into this cell on Monday afternoon, October 21, 1835, to save him from the violence of a respectable and influential mob, who sought to destroy him for preaching the abominable and dangerous doctrine that all men are created equal, and that all oppression is odious in the sight of God."[11]

DEATH AND IMPRISONMENT

It is unknown how many advocates of abolition were threatened by mobs during this tense period, but mob violence was always a danger and could sometimes result in death. In 1837, Elijah Lovejoy became a victim of mob violence for his work as the editor of the *Observer*, an antislavery newspaper published in Alton, Illinois. Three times he bought a new press; three times his new press was thrown into the river by mobs. Lovejoy appealed to the citizens of the town to support a person's right to freedom of speech. "If civil authorities refuse to protect me," he said, "I must look to God, and if I die I am determined to make my grave in Alton."[12]

60

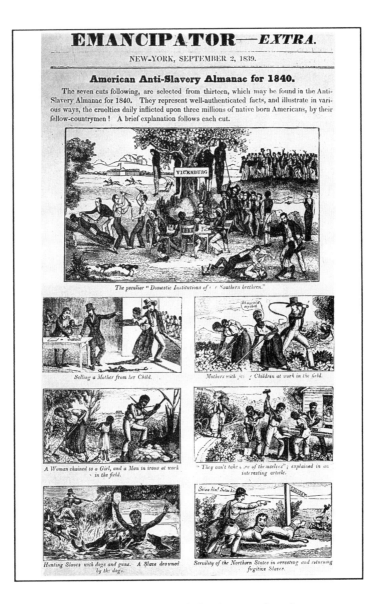

The front page of the September 2, 1839, issue of the antislavery newspaper *Emancipator* featured seven woodcuts illustrating the cruelties inflicted on slaves.

Some of Alton's citizens were outraged and vowed to protect the editor's freedom of speech. When the fourth press arrived, fifty of Alton's supporters showed up and vowed to help him protect it. They guarded the press around the clock. The next evening a mob arrived and demanded the press. The building was set on fire. The citizens beat the mob away by firing pistol shots and the fire was put out. Suddenly, it became very quiet. Lovejoy slowly opened the front door to see if the mob was gone. A flurry of gunfire erupted. Lovejoy staggered back into the building and died from bullet wounds.

Imprisonment was also a danger for workers of the Underground Railroad, and some entered cells never to be released. Charles Torren was arrested in 1843 for helping slaves escape and was sentenced to the penitentiary for six years. He wrote to a friend, "If I am a guilty man, I am a very guilty one; for I have aided nearly four hundred slaves to escape to freedom, the greater part of whom would probably, but for my exertions, have died in slavery."[13] While in prison, Torren's health deteriorated and he died on May 9, 1846.

Another worker who died in prison was Seth Concklin of Philadelphia. Concklin offered to go into the South to rescue the family of Peter Still, a slave who had escaped from Alabama. Concklin and the runaways were captured in Indiana. When Still's former master arrived to claim them, he had Concklin chained. It was the last time Concklin was seen alive. He was later found drowned, his hands and feet still bound in chains.

Because of the secrecy required of the Underground Railroad, it is impossible to calculate the total cost of its labor. It is impossible to calculate the physical harm done to the workers or the number of lives lost to the cause of helping slaves escape. Whatever the numbers, it can probably be said that hardly any of the conductors resented the hardships of—or thought the price too steep for—bringing so many souls to freedom.

FIVE
RIDING THE RAILS
TO FREEDOM

But if a fugitive claim your help on this journey,
break the law and give it him. . . . Feed him, clothe
him, harbor him, by day and by night, and conceal
him from his pursuers and from the
officers of the law.
—Charles Beecher, in "The Duty of Disobedience to
Wicked Laws," a sermon on the Fugitive Slave Law,
1851[1]

The secret, or "underground" methods of rescuing runaway slaves were already known as early as 1804, but the
number or routes a rescue could take was limited because
the number of people helping was limited. By 1850,
however, the northern states were covered by numerous
lines of the Underground Railroad and the South was
declaring enormous losses because of these lines.

CHOICE OF ROUTES

Because secrecy was so vital, and safety was more important than quickness, the routes were far from direct. They
usually zigzagged. Sometimes a number of routes were
available; the decision as to which routes to use was
usually left up to the local conductors. Each guide had a
favorite route, but he or she might also have a choice
between two or more routes—for instance, the right-
handed road would lead to one station; the left-handed
road to another. A guide who felt that danger was immi-
nent might switch to a different route for a change or
even go back over the same road to confuse anyone following him, skip a station, or go the long way around.

TESTING THE ROUTES

Before starting out, Underground Railroad workers sometimes might test the roads first. They would send out a carriage or wagon containing an Underground Railroad worker and a group of free blacks with the proper papers. If anyone were watching the road, they would swoop down on the carriage, thinking the free blacks were fugitives. The Underground Railroad workers would then know they should use another route for escaped slaves. Or they just might find a hiding place and sit and wait for a while.

It sometimes took days or even months before the danger was over and a group could start out again. One time, a reward of $2,200 was offered for a group of fugitives from a Kentucky plantation. A large posse of slave catchers had been sent after them and was watching almost every road. For three days and nights, the conductor steered them from field to field, from station to station, trying to break the blockade the slave catchers had set up. Sometimes he even backtracked to a house they had already hidden in, but the slave catchers were persistent.

The Underground workers conferred around a table by candlelight. Long into the night they talked, trying to figure out a route that would be safe. On the third night, a horse galloped up to the door. It was a pro-slavery neighbor who was playing host to the slave catchers. The Underground group nervously let him into the house.

"When dark comes," he told his surprised neighbors, "just take them across the woods to my house. They [the slave catchers] will never suspect me of having anything to do with carrying them away, for I'm feeding the catchers."

The workers decided to trust the neighbor and at 2:00 A.M. they made their way through the mud and rain. The fugitives stayed upstairs while the slave catchers took their meals and slept downstairs. The next evening, the conductor finally broke through the blockade and led his little group to safety without ever knowing why the neighbor had changed his views.[2]

THE RAILROAD SYSTEM

Because new lines constantly were being formed and old ones contantly were being temporarily or permanently abandoned, it is impossible to estimate how many lines were in operation at one time. Some lines were in operation in Pennsylvania, Illinois, and Vermont in the 1820s, but as new communities developed in the North, so did new lines. These routes spread to New Hampshire and Massachusetts in the 1830s and were soon criss-crossing the entire northeastern section of the United States. (See map on pages 66–67.)

It wasn't until after the Civil War that writers began to interview people willing to admit they had been part of the Underground Railroad. Then the writers started to piece together the routes and make maps that showed all the possibilities. Until then the routes were mostly secret.

The researchers found that the system usually ran from Kentucky and Virginia across Ohio or from Maryland through Pennsylvania and New York to Canada. This did not mean that the other states did not participate. Many states were said to be covered with stations and routes not found in regular railway guides or on regular maps.

There seemed to be two factors involved in establishing an Underground Railroad route–geographical location and availability of Underground workers in an area. For instance, there were fewer stations in Iowa, even though it bordered on slave territory, because it was newly developed. This meant it might be a long distance between stations. Ohio, on the other hand, had at least twenty main lines because not only did it have a larger population with less distance between stops, it also had

65

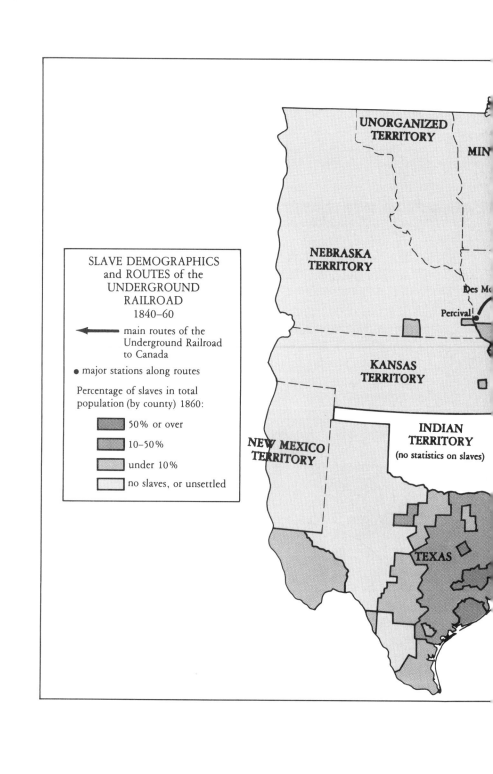

SLAVE DEMOGRAPHICS
and ROUTES of the
UNDERGROUND
RAILROAD
1840–60

⬅ main routes of the
Underground Railroad
to Canada

● major stations along routes

Percentage of slaves in total
population (by county) 1860:

50% or over

10–50%

under 10%

no slaves, or unsettled

UNORGANIZED
TERRITORY

MIN

NEBRASKA
TERRITORY

Des Mo

Percival

KANSAS
TERRITORY

INDIAN
TERRITORY
(no statistics on slaves)

NEW MEXICO
TERRITORY

TEXAS

CANADA

MAINE

Montreal

WISCONSIN

MICH.

Collingwood

Montpelier

N.Y.

VT.

N.H.

Portland

Amherstburg

Rochester

Oswego

Boston

Providence

Port Huron

Dresden

Albany

MASS.

Milwaukee

Detroit

Erie

CONN.

R.I.

New London

IOWA

Cassopolis

Cleveland

Franklin

PA

Jersey

New Haven

Chicago

IND.

Toledo

Shippenville

City

New York

Davenport

Ottawa

OHIO

New

Clearfield

Phoenixville

Philadelphia

Springfield

ILLINOIS

Columbus

Castle

Uniontown

N.J.

Quincy

Newport

Indianapolis

Cumberland

DEL.

Chester

Salem

Cincinnati

Marietta

VIRGINIA

Leavenworth

Ripley

Ironton

MISSOURI

Evansville

Jeffersonville

Norfolk

Cairo

KENTUCKY

NORTH

CAROLINA

New Bern

ARKANSAS

TENNESSEE

SOUTH

CAROLINA

MISS.

Charleston

ALABAMA

GEORGIA

LOUISIANA

FLA.

0   100   200

rivers with numerous tributaries for quick and convenient travel. Its borders with Kentucky, a slave state, had about 160 miles (257 km) of river frontage.

Some communities for reasons of location or the extent of their development, never had routes on the Underground Railroad, or were involved very little, despite their eagerness to help. Some towns saw only one or two fugitives during the entire period before the Civil War. Residents of Lynn, Massachusetts, were eager to help, but never got the chance because no fugitives ever came their way. Still, they held mock slave hunts to "practice." A "burly member" of the community impersonated the slave hunter and the others practiced outwitting or overpowering him.

The other factor involved in the development of routes—the availability of workers—also was involved in making Ohio one of the most popular routes. Many communities of Quakers and antislavery southerners had made their homes in that state. Ohio also contained institutions such as Oberlin College, Western Reserve College, and Geneva College, which were dedicated to helping the slaves to freedom. In addition to white settlers, blacks who found their way to Ohio remained in the state and were willing to help other blacks who came afterward. Finally, the Ottawa Indians of Ohio were known to be some of the earliest friends of black refugees.

Because of the large number of Quakers living in Pennsylvania and because of its easy access to New York, that state was also a popular route for Underground work. Philadelphia had a route that ran overland across New Jersey to Jersey City and New York. Refugees reaching Uniontown in southwestern Pennsylvania from Virginia and Maryland were sent to Pittsburgh, then to Cleveland by rail or along the Allegheny or the Ohio river and its tributaries north. West of the Susquehanna River, Gettysburg and York were stations used mostly by slaves escaping from Maryland. Other fugitives were sent along the eastern shore of the Chesapeake River, passing north-ward until they crossed the Susquehanna to stations in Lancaster and Chester counties in eastern Pennsylvania.

SAMPLE UNDERGROUND ROUTES

Western Pennsylvania was dotted with a variety of "safe houses" and small towns on the Underground Railroad route. One such route began at the station at Crowe's Mills on the line between Virginia and Greene County, Pennsylvania. From there, the slaves were transported to the home of Isaac Teagarden on Wheeling Creek, then to the farm of Joseph Gray near Graysville, where they were concealed in a wooden ravine in view of the road.

From Graysville, it took three hours to get to the next station, Kenneth McCoy's farm at West Alexander. When this place became known to slave hunters, the station was changed to the Bell farm nearby or to a two-story frame house at the foot of Coon Island Hill on the National Pike (or road). From there it was 12 miles (19.3 km) to Middleton. From Middleton the fugitives then took one of the New York routes into Canada.

An Underground Railroad route between New Jersey and New York might possibly begin at a house some 20 miles (32 km) from Philadelphia called Station A. The horses were changed after the hectic ride and the fugitives were sent off to Station B in a town called Bordentown. From Bordentown, they were taken to Princeton and then to New Brunswick.

The fugitives might have trouble crossing the Raritan River on the way because of slave hunters, so Under-ground Railroad workers made arrangements with Cornelius Cornell who lived on the outskirts of New Brunswick to warn them when slave catchers or spies were at the regular crossing. If they were, the route to New York City would be changed. Once in the city, they made their way to the Forty-Second Street Station

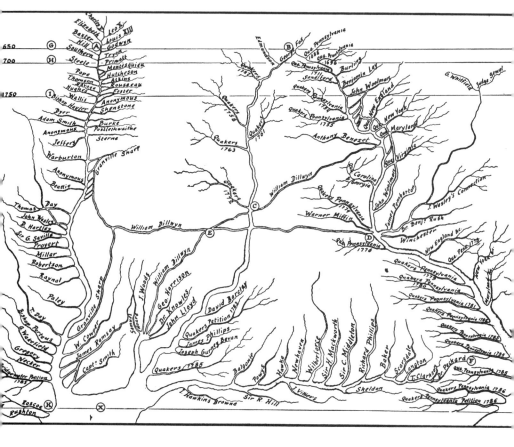

The names of Underground agents flourish like tree
branches in this map entitled "Stream of
Abolition," published in London in 1808.

(later known as Grand Central Station), where they bought tickets for Syracuse on the real railroad and from there made their way into Canada.

The length of time it took to travel these routes varied—it took one slave a year to get from Alabama to Ohio. Another Alabama slave traveled 1,200 miles (1,931 km), eating roots and wild berries, before he got to Pennsylvania. The length of time it took depended on many factors: the proximity of a slave catcher or owner, the route, the weather, and the mode of transportation—by water, foot, or on actual railroads.

WATER ROUTES

Underground Railroad workers employed any means they could to transport their charges along the escape routes. As one worker, Calvin Fairbanks, said:

> Forty-seven slaves I guided toward the north star, in violation of the state codes of Virginia and Kentucky. I piloted them through the forests, mostly by night; girls, fair and white, dressed as ladies; men and boys as gentlemen, or servants; men in women's clothes, and women in men's clothes; boys dressed as girls, and girls as boys; on foot, on horseback, in buggies, carriages, common wagons, in and under loads of hay, straw, old furniture, boxes and bags; crossing the Jordan of the slave, swimming or wading chin deep; or in boats or skiffs, on rafts, and often on a pine log. And I never suffered one to be recaptured.[3]

Traveling by waterway was one of the fastest means of escape for the slaves. The pro-slavery people knew this and tried to put a stop to it. As early as 1726, masters of vessels in Virginia had to swear they would make a diligent search of their craft to prevent stowaway slaves.

71

Later, slaves secured passage either secretly or with the ship master's consent. Most sailed from southern ports to the shores of New England, landing in such places as New Haven, New Bedford, Boston, Norfolk, Portsmouth, and other ports.

The mighty Ohio River was a favorite route for escaping slaves, but it could be an enemy as well as friend. A slave often made his or her way to the river only to find there was no way to cross. He or she might be captured while desperately searching for a skiff or small boat that had broken loose from its mooring. Many slaves had never lived near water and knew nothing about navigating rivers or controlling boats. It will never be known how many lost their lives trying to reach freedom on the other side. They did learn, however, that the best time to cross the river was in winter. Then the river froze over and they could walk across the ice.

One such dramatic escape involved a slave woman named Eliza Harris, the same Eliza immortalized in *Uncle Tom's Cabin*. Eliza Harris's owner had fallen on hard times and the rumor reached Eliza that she was going to be sold. Even though it was the middle of winter, she bundled up their youngest child and ran away.

Throughout the night, Eliza made her way toward the Ohio River and the promise of freedom. At daylight, she arrived on the Ohio's bank at the Ripley crossing. She was dismayed to find that parts of the frozen river had melted and were drifting downstream in the form of huge ice floes. She took refuge with a sympathetic Scottish couple who lived nearby. They advised her to wait until night when it was colder and the river had re-frozen. She was told that, after crossing the river, a "good man" on the other side of the river would help her to freedom.

That night Eliza made her way back to the riverbank. But her spirits failed. The river was still not frozen. As she stood, uncertain of what to do next, she heard a commotion. Horrified, she recognized the sounds of blood-

72

hounds on the scent. The dreaded slave hunters appeared on the horizon. Panic-stricken, she wrapped her baby in her shawl and leapt onto the closest floe. Then she leapt to the next. Slowly she made her way across the ice floes. The "good man" on the other side of the river, the Reverend John Ripley, had been alerted by the noise of the hounds and watched in horror as she slipped into the icy waters several times when the floes tipped under her weight. Her clothes were drenched and her hands, clutching her wailing baby, were numb from the cold. Finally, she was close enough to the shore for the reverend to reach out and pull her up onto free soil.

The story of Eliza's dramatic escape became quite controversial when it was recounted in *Uncle Tom's Cabin*. Northerners were outraged that such horrors could occur; southerners said such a person never existed. The debate continued for years and people like Taylor Brownlee came forward to say the story was indeed true. She remembered her father, James Taylor, running an Underground Railroad station at his farm near Iberia, Ohio. She recalled how Eliza was brought to her father's house and remained there for several days until it was safe to go on. She said:

> All the Taylor family was familiar with the story of how Eliza had escaped from Kentucky by crossing the Ohio River in the ice with the slave hunters at her heels and when *Uncle Tom's Cabin* appeared some time later they at once recognized the incident. [4]

Some slaves were lucky enough to escape by steamboat and thus circumvent the dangers Eliza endured. One way of transporting the slaves to safety on a steamboat was to pay for an entire stateroom to a free port and get the key to the room. Shortly before the boat left, amidst the hustle and bustle on the wharf, the conductor would bring the fugitives on board as if they were servants carrying the baggage of the master or mistress.

Once the fugitives were safely in the stateroom, the conductor put the key on the inside of the door and the slaves locked themselves in. If the stateroom was paid for, no ship's officer or servant was allowed to go into the room. Then the conductor telegraphed the next port of their arrival, and when the boat docked there would be another conductor to meet them.

Levi Coffin often received notices like "Go to box seventy-two, at the post office, and take charge of my letters or papers, which you will find there." Or "pay forty-three dollars to Dr. Peck on my account."[5] Coffin knew this was a secret code for the number of a stateroom on a steamboat and often boasted how the Underground Railroad had rescued twenty-seven slaves this way during one spring and summer.

Although travel by water seemed the safest way to transport slaves quickly, there were often men who preyed on the helpless passengers. Some seamen, William Still said, "would bring any kind of freight that would pay the most."[6] One captain would not make the trip from Richmond to Philadelphia unless he had three passengers at a hundred dollars each. A slave in Norfolk paid a ship's captain a hundred dollars to take him north. The captain gave the money to the slave's owner instead—for a $25 reward.

One of the most dramatic stories of how men sometimes took advantage of slaves for money was the tale of Eliza Wilson. Eliza worked on a plantation near New Orleans when she fell in love with John Wilson, a white machinist. Eliza and John had two children and when the owner became fearful that John might try to help Eliza escape, he sent her 14 miles (22.5 km) away. She was forbidden to communicate with John on threat of his death. Wilson, meanwhile, made arrangements with the officers of a boat bound for Cincinnati to help Eliza escape, and he eventually got her on board. He paid another passenger $200 to help her make the trip to freedom.

Unfortunately, the man Wilson had paid was a gambler and he gambled her passage money away on the voyage. When they docked, he told her she was in a free state and could go where she pleased. Then he walked down the gangplank and disappeared.

The captain was furious when he found out she had no money for her passage. Suspecting she was a runaway slave, he was preparing to put her into a skiff to row her across the river to Kentucky, where he would sell her for the passage money. A black steward overheard the plan and sped to the home of a lawyer friend. The lawyer contacted Levi Coffin and they had the boat captain hauled into court. The court agreed that Eliza could go free if Levi would pay the steamboat fare.

Nor were white men the only ones who took advantage of the escaping slaves' plights. Free blacks also helped slaves escape by water—for a fee. Anthony Bingey paid $400 for such a guide to take a group partway through Ohio. But the *Voice of the Fugitive*, an antislavery newspaper, warned, "If any professed friend refuses to aid you or your friends in making their escape from Slavery, unless they be paid an extravagant price for it, they are not to be trusted; no matter whether they are white or black." They gave an example of a free black who got $50 to $300 to help slaves escape. If a slave hunter offered more, "the poor fugitive would be betrayed and dragged back into a living death."[7]

Several factors made travel by water popular among escaping slaves. Northerners owned many of the steamboats plying southern rivers and rivers dividing the North from the South. They also ran their crafts on the great network of inland rivers.

Since the South was not as industrialized as the North, a large majority of river workers—mechanics, steamboat officers, and clerks—were usually northerners. Steamboats also used large quantities of wood, and the men who sold the wood were usually northerners. The northern workers, in turn, hired slaves to load the wood so it was not uncommon to see Negro slaves straining up the gangplanks in the South, struggling under the weight of a load of wood. It was also not uncommon, if someone were watching closely from the shore, to notice that not every slave who went up the gangplank came back down the gangplank. Finally, when the wood was all loaded, the steamship would start slowly down the river, carrying among its passengers, five or six runaways, on their way to freedom.

The Underground workers who used the waterways knew that besides booking passage, getting runaways on board as workers was one of the best ways to help them escape. To try to sneak aboard was almost impossible; to try to row out to a boat in a skiff or swim hidden by a floating log meant risking the danger of the huge paddle wheels.

Not all slaves used the huge steamboats for their escapes. They used anything that floated, from small scows and sailboats to logs and floating debris—anything that would take them to free soil. For instance, a crossing at the Ohio River, midway between Owensboro, Kentucky, and Rockport, Indiana, provided a variety of floating vessels on which to escape. There was a fisherman's hut on the south bank of the river. Two men sold their fish to steamboats, flatboats, and coal fleets. On the side, they negotiated with the mariners to carry refugees across the Ohio on the smaller boats.

Another favorite place to escape by water was on Lake Michigan, where antislavery people owned an unpretentious lumber bark that looked as if it couldn't travel 5 miles (8 km) from shore, much less up and down the giant lake. The antislavery crew cruised along the shore, loading and unloading freight, including escaped slaves.

Slaves board a paddle wheeler at
Vicksburg, Mississippi, bound for the West.

When canals, such as the Erie Canal, were completed, other avenues of escape for fugitives were opened. Escaping slaves paid for passage on the slow-moving boats if they had the money; if not, they followed the towpaths that ran alongside the canals. They found these routes, since they were new, to be much safer than the heavily used older roads.

ESCAPE BY ROAD

If a waterway was not available, or if the waterways were being watched, fugitives followed the Underground Railroad routes on foot, on horseback, in buggies, carriages, covered wagons, and open wagons, in and under loads of hay, grain, straw, old furniture, boxes, bags, and even pigs. On one of Harriet Tubman's trips, she and her group of slaves were placed in a long wagon belonging to bricklayers. They were told to lie down flat. Then boards were placed over them and bricks were placed on top of the boards for the journey out of the town. One slave complained that it was like being in a coffin.

One Underground Railroad worker, a bookbinder from Troy, Ohio, had a large wagon built with drawers, so he had a large hiding place in the center of the wagon's bed. Abram Allen, a Quaker in Oakland, Ohio, had a special three-seated wagon made for carrying fugitives. He

Braving the perils of the road: Fugitive slaves, above, cross into Union lines in an ancient farm wagon called a schooner. Below: Bounty hunters and slave owners tracked the flight of slaves, sometimes shooting them on sight.

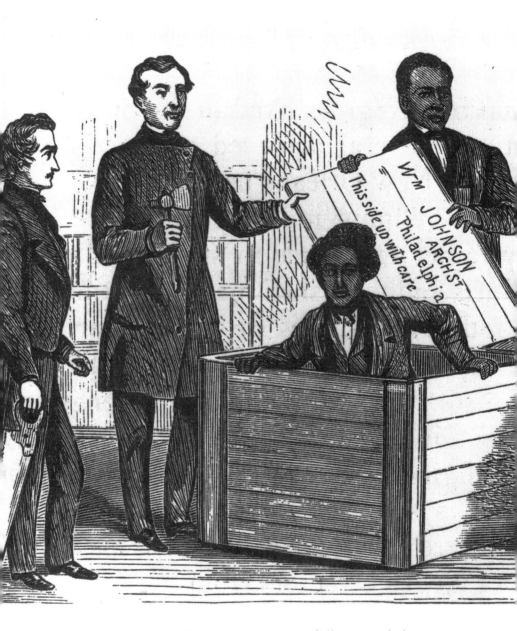

Henry "Box" Brown was successfully smuggled
to freedom, thanks to a wooden crate.

called it the Liberator. It was curtained all around and was large enough to hold eight to ten people. It had a mechanism with a bell, which recorded the number of miles traveled, so the anxious slaves inside would know how far they had gone and how far they still had to go to the next safe house.

Underground Railroad workers often called upon traveling families to take a slave along the route to the next depot. Some families were afraid of being caught, but they might agree to let the slave follow the trail they had left. The slave would travel by night. Most slaves knew "their" wagon's tracks and sometimes the families left signals. If they came to a forked road, for instance, they might turn down the branches of a nearby bush to indicate which road they had taken.

The slave would then approach the family's camp the next morning before daylight and get breakfast and provisions for the day. The day was spent hiding in the bushes or thickets and getting some sleep before it was time to continue the journey that night. If the family came to a river that was crossed by a ferry, they waited for the slave, hid him or her in the wagon just long enough to get to the other side, then continued on their dangerous journey.

ESCAPE AS BAGGAGE

One of the most interesting, but dangerous, ways slaves made their way along Underground Railroad routes was as baggage. On a few occasions, boxes and chests were used to transport the slaves along with other freight. One young pregnant woman was boxed up by a friend and sent by freight to Philadelphia. She was left overnight in one depot and turned upside down more than once. Her friend, meanwhile, arrived in Philadelphia ahead of her and made arrangements for the box to be delivered to a Mrs. Myers, an Underground Railroad worker. When the box arrived there were no noises from inside; the women feared the worst. Mrs. Myers called a neighbor in and the two pried off the lid. The woman on the straw of the box lay still, but she was breathing. She was weak and frightened, but alive.

Another fugitive got his nickname from being mailed in a box and shipped as freight to Philadelphia. Henry "Box" Brown was placed in a box 2 feet, 8 inches deep by 3 feet (.8 by .9m) long. The box was then nailed up and hooped with five hickory hoops around the outside. The box was marked "This side up with care" and sent along to Philadelphia.

Despite the cautionary sign, Henry often found himself upside down on the long journey as the box was moved from dray to train to ferry to wagon. One time he was upside down for 20 miles (32 km) until, he said, the veins in his temples "were swollen to the thickness of his finger and beat like hammers."[8]

Twenty-six hours later, Henry arrived at his destination, the Anti-Slavery Society offices in Philadelphia. The committee members were uneasy. Suppose there were a dead man inside the box now instead of the live slave they have been expecting? Cautiously, one of the committee members rapped on the box.

"All right?" he asked.

"All right, sir," came the reply.

The elated men used a saw and hatchet to the box, and out stepped Brown.

"How do you do, gentlemen?" were his first words.[9]

ESCAPE BY RAILROAD

Although the Underground Railroad was an imaginary railroad, it often used the real railroads to transport slaves to freedom. (The workers called these "surface lines.") Railroads like the Providence and Worcester and the Vermont Central railroads, the Reading Railroad and the Mad River Railroad in Ohio provided transportation if a slave wasn't being closely pursued. (Workers didn't like to use the railroad otherwise if there was any chance of being trapped with no way to escape.)

Railroad employees who were sympathetic to the plight of the slaves helped with their escape. Some of them were also conductors on the Underground Railroad. I. Newton Pierce, an Underground Railroad conductor, had an understanding with the real conductors on the Cleveland and Western Railroad from Alliance to Cleveland that blacks holding tickets with his initials, "I.N.P.," were to be admitted to the train without question unless slave catchers were thought to be on board.

The refugees, especially those of light color, were often dressed in good clothes and carried tickets they had purchased for their trip on the railroad. Others had to ride in baggage cars or on freight trains, which provided more safety. If word came that a station was being watched, the freight train could be stopped anywhere between stations and the runaways could scatter into the woods or find a safe house until they could continue on their journey. No one but the crew would know the train had stopped. The train could also make unscheduled stops to take on fugitives who were hiding along the way.

One of the most exciting railway escapes involved the volatile John Fairfield. One of his favorite tricks was to dress light-colored slaves in wigs and powder their faces to make them look as if they were white. On a trip from Harpers Ferry in Virginia, he used the express train bound for Pittsburgh. Unfortunately, the slaves were missed almost immediately and their owner rented a railroad engine and one car. Off he took in full pursuit down the tracks after the train carrying his slaves. The owner overtook the train just as it reached Pittsburgh. The fugitives looked out the window and saw the other train. Guessing they were being pursued, they jumped off the slowly moving train and ran in different directions. Not one was recaptured and Fairfield was able to get them to freedom. Levi Coffin later said that a friend had written him that "Fairfield had just reached there with the best looking company of fugitives that had ever passed through Detroit."[10]

These journeys were often desperate and fear-filled. They were carried out in tortuous heat and freezing cold. Despite the terrible discomfort and danger involved in traveling on the Underground Railroad, it is doubtful that many complained. They knew that at the end of the line, freedom waited.

SIX

THE ART OF "TRAVELING THE RAILS"

If you come to us, and are hungry, we will feed you; if thirsty, we will give you drink, if naked, we will clothe you; if sick, we will minister to your necessities; if in prison, we will visit you; if you need a hiding-place from the face of pursuers, we will provide one that even bloodhounds will not scent out.
—Credo of the American Anti-Slavery Society[1]

During the early years of the Underground Railroad, slaves were simply given directions to the next safe house and told to follow the North Star. Escape was often a matter of going from one Quaker family to the next until safety was reached. However, as the Underground Railroad expanded and became more organized, workers guided the slaves themselves and became involved in a war of wits to see how they could trick the southern slave owners.

IGNORANCE OF ROUTES

Slave owners kept their slaves as ignorant of the Underground escape routes—and of the world in general—as they possibly could. Few slaves had traveled more than a few miles from their plantations, and many were terrified to leave the safety of the area, no matter how terrible it was, for fear of the unknown. An abolitionist talking to an escaped slave in 1843 found that the slave did not know where he had been raised or the names of any of the places he had gone through while escaping. William Johnson, a runaway who had fled from Virginia, had been told that the Detroit River was over 3,000 miles (4,884 km) wide and that if a ship started out at night, it would find itself "right where she started from" the next day. Frederick Douglass said, "The real distance was great enough, but the imagined distance was, to our ignorance, much greater. Slaveholders sought to impress their slaves with a belief in the boundlessness of slave territory, and of their own limitless power. Our notions of the geography of the country were very vague and indistinct."[2]

He also said, "We had heard of Canada...simply as a country to which the wild goose and the swan repaired at the end of winter to escape the heat of summer, but not as the home of man."[3]

A good example of how some slaves knew precious little of geography was an incident involving twenty-six Maryland fugitive slaves who arrived in Pennsylvania in 1842. They thought they were in Canada, free and safe. They walked down the streets in broad daylight in large numbers. They had been told since childhood to beware of the "white man," so they were afraid to talk to anyone. Finally, suspecting they were fugitives, a group of antislavery residents warned them of the dangers. They insisted the fugitives break up into smaller groups and hide until Underground Railroad workers could lead them to Canada.

SPREADING THE WORD

To combat the ignorance of many slaves, northern workers tried to communicate the nature of their services to the blacks still in bondage. They raised money to run off thousands of "scatter sheets" or antislavery pamphlets. They left these sheets on roadsides, in barrooms, stage coaches, and railway cars.

Some Underground workers thought that publicizing the Underground Railroad's services was more important than secrecy. They began to use the newspapers to spread the word that the Underground Railroad was available to those slaves who wanted to hop on board to freedom. In 1844, for example, the Chicago *Western Citizen* quoted G.W. Burke, an Underground "Superintendent," as saying that "the U.R.R. is in excellent order. The station keepers and superintendents are all active and trust-worthy men, [and] chattels intrusted to their care will be forwarded with great care, and unparalleled speed."[4]

In 1852, a Columbus paper printed a letter stating the "underground railroad, and especially the express train, is doing good business just now." It complimented the conductors and warned it "would not be very safe for slave-catchers to get on the track when the bell rings, at some of the depots in Northern Ohio."[5]

In 1854, a Baraboo, Wisconsin, paper let everyone know the progress of the Underground Railroad. "The road is partly completed," the article ran, using a real railroad as an analogy. "But as yet we have nothing but wooden rails, and our cars are drawn by horse power, as we have not yet procured our steam engine."[6]

Some northern workers, knowing they had the law on their side, became quite brave in advertising their services. William Stedman wrote a letter in December 1850 to the Cleveland *Daily True Democrat* to let everyone know he was the local "agent" for smuggling fugitives into Canada. In a Syracuse, New York, newspaper, the Reverend J. W. Loguen, an ex-slave, announced in 1850 that he would be helping fugitives and maintaining the city's Underground Railroad depot. Any fugitives taking that route could get in touch with him, he said.

In addition to letting readers know that their services were available and that they were doing well, publicity was also designed to get the public excited and to taunt slaveholders by describing the large numbers of slaves who had supposedly escaped on the Underground Railroad. The Louisville *Daily Courier* estimated that in one week alone Cleveland workers had transported $20,000 worth of property, and the *Richmond Enquirer* said in 1859 that Detroit had dispatched ninety-four fugitives, estimated to be worth $94,000, to Canada. The Burlington (Vermont) *Tribune* even published notices of the arrival and departure of fugitives so that slaveholders would see that their slaves had escaped to Canada and call off their searches.

As the success of the Railroad escalated, workers became more confident and bold. "We can run a lot of slaves into Canada within 48 hours," taunted Henry Bib, in the Canadian newspaper called *The Voice of the Fugitive*, "and we defy the slaveholders and their abettors to beat that if they can." He called the South "the land of whips and chains," but Canada was the land where "the people are all free, the climate is mild, the soil is rich and productive, and the markets are ready and advantageous to the farmer." He warned them they were wasting their money by hiring bloodhounds and "negro hunters."[7]

Even reports of unsuccessful rescues might be used to get public sympathy. In December 1858, the government indicted thirty-seven people from Oberlin, Ohio, who had been involved in a rescue a few months earlier. The trial received a vast amount of publicity, and thousands of people attended a mass rally in the yard of the Cleveland jail where the prisoners were housed. When the prisoners were returned to Oberlin, 2,000 people came to greet them. Bells rang, bonfires lined the streets, and 300 supporters waited at the church to hear brief speeches, including one by the Cleveland sheriff, who had befriended the prisoners.

Not everyone was happy about the publicity received by the Underground Railroad. Most workers, fearful for their safety and that of their families, had maintained strict secrecy. Frederick Douglass once complained:

I have never approved of the very public manner, in which some of our western friends

88

have conducted what they call the "Underground Railroad," but which, I think, by their open declarations has been made emphatically, the Upper-ground Railroad. Its stations are far better known to the slave-holders than to the slaves.[8]

Others pointed out that only a few slaves could read and those who did read rarely had access to antislavery publications. Instead, they would be given only certain "safe" material aimed at convincing them that it was impossible to escape. These "safe" materials reported recaptures and stories of terrible punishments that were inflicted on the slaves who tried to escape.

SECRET CODES

Underground Railroad workers recognized an urgent need to communicate information secretly and safely to those slaves who were not allowed to read antislavery material or who couldn't read. Ingenious ways to reach their audience were soon developed. The workers smuggled handkerchiefs printed with antislavery pictures into bales of goods headed for southern markets. They became expert at sending and decoding messages. Workers in Philadelphia assigned code numbers to their stations—10 was the code for Pennsylvania, 20 for Seville, Ohio, and 27 for Medina, Ohio. Cleveland was called "Hope," Sandusky was called "Sunrise." A slave might receive a letter saying the "good ship Zion" was soon to arrive, a signal it was time to escape.

Business letters between Underground Railroad workers often contained codes for other "business." When I. Newton Pierce sent fugitives from Alliance, Ohio, to Cleveland, they carried a note to a Cleveland merchant in the Underground, saying: "Please forward immediately to the U.G. baggage this day sent to you." In

89

another example, a message from G.W. Weston in Iowa to his friend C.B. Campbell of Clinton read:

Mr. C.B.C.:

Dear Sir: By to-morrow evening's mail, you will receive two volumes of the "Irrespressible Conflict" bound in black. After perusal, please forward, and oblige,

Yours truly,

G.W.W. [9]

These coded letters sometimes contained the terms southerners used in describing blacks. For instance, Pierce wrote, "I sent thee two bales of black wool," meaning that he would be sending two slaves. [10] "Black wool" referred to the terms people used to describe black hair.

Levi Coffin once sent a message which reflected the fact that some slaveholders thought African-Americans had no souls, but were a species of baboon. It said:

Shipped in good form and well conditioned, two baboons of fine stock and very valuable. Please receive and forward the same to George D. Baptist, Detroit, Michigan, by way of Camden and Fort Wayne; I consider that to be the safest route. Take special care of them; do not allow them to run at large. They are quite tame, but bloodhounds sometimes get on their track and might injure them. They are male and female; the female is not very stout at present, having just recovered from a spell of sickness. Please give them a warm dry place in which to lie, while at Winchester, and do not let them be too much exposed to idle spectators, as it might annoy them. They will be of little trouble about feeding, as they eat the same kind of food that human beings do, and seem to thrive on it. Put them in charge of a good conductor, who will take special care of them. [11]

Harriet Tubman, who could neither read nor write, often used letters to communicate with those slaves she intended to bring out of the South by asking someone to write the letters for her. One time she began to worry about three of her own brothers she had left behind in Maryland. She kept dreaming that they had been sold and put on a chain gang, a work force where slaves were chained together to keep them from escaping. At that time, she was making two trips a year into the South to rescue slaves, one in the fall and one in the spring. She decided to alert her brothers that she would take them out on her next fall trip in 1850.

Harriet had a friend write a letter to Jacob Jackson, a free African-American who lived near the plantation where two of her brothers worked. She had the friend pretend the letter was from Jacob's adopted son, William Henry. The letter arrived in Maryland, and as was the custom when letters were received from the North, the postmaster opened and read it. It said:

"Read my letter to the old folks, and give my love to them, and tell my brothers to be always watching unto prayer, and when the good old ship Zion comes along, to be ready to step on board."

The postmaster knew it was a secret message, but he couldn't figure it out. William Henry Jackson had no brothers and sisters; he was an orphan and had no "old folks." The postmaster sent for Jacob. When he was questioned about the letter, Jacob played dumb. Despite being an excellent reader, he read the letter very slowly, following each letter with his finger.

"That letter can't be meant for me nohow," he said, after he had memorized the message. "I can't make head or tail of it."[12]

After he left the postmaster, Jacob delivered the message to Harriet's brothers. The following fall Harriet kept her promise. She not only brought her own brothers, but three other slaves, to freedom.

Sometimes messages were hidden in the words of

songs, especially Negro spirituals. One famous conductor who used songs to carry his message to the slaves was a man who went by the name of Peg Leg Joe. Peg Leg was a former sailor who worked for hire at plantations as a handyman. While there he made friends with the slaves and taught them what appeared to be a harmless song called "Follow the Drinking Gourd." (See lyrics on page 93.)

Actually, the lyrics to "Follow the Drinking Gourd" contained hidden directions to the Underground Railroad. The drinking gourd referred to the Big Dipper, which points to the North Star. Once Peg Leg Joe had taught the slaves this song, he moved on, marking the way for those who decided to follow by drawing a peg foot in charcoal on dead trees.

Like Peg Leg Joe's song, most communication was best delivered by word of mouth. The most effective messengers were those whose work required traveling especially in the South – people such as salesmen, preachers, and mechanics. Dr. Alexander M. Ross, a Canadian physician and naturalist who had received decorations of knighthood from several European monarchs for his scientific work, was quite adept at spreading the word of the Underground Railroad. As he wandered through the fields and woods taking notes on birds (his specialty), he was able to talk with the slaves, and provide them with money and instructions on how to escape. Whenever he left an area, large numbers of slaves disappeared soon afterward.

Because the slaves often had to travel long distances by themselves before reaching an Underground Railroad station, messages also had to be transmitted instructing them how to travel safely. They needed to know how to spot signals that meant a house was safe, and which signals would gain them entry to those houses. A quilt hanging on the clothesline with a house and smoking chimney among its designs meant this was a safe house. A house whose chimney had a ring of white bricks

Follow the Drinking Gourd

Chorus:
Follow the drinking gourd!
Follow the drinking gourd.
For the old man is awaiting
for to carry you to freedom
If you follow the drinking gourd.
When the sun comes back,
and the first quail calls,
Follow the drinking gourd.
For the old man is awaiting
for to carry you to freedom
If you follow the drinking gourd.

(Repeat chorus)
The riverbank makes a very good road,
The dead trees will show you the way.
Left foot, peg foot, traveling on,
Follow the drinking gourd.

(Repeat chorus)
When the great big river meets the little river,
Follow the drinking gourd.
For the old man is a-waiting for to carry you to freedom
If you follow the drinking gourd.

(Repeat chorus)
The river ends between two hills,
Follow the drinking gourd.
There's another river on the other side,
Follow the drinking gourd.

around the top meant the house was safe. No signal was too simple for these "grapevine telegraphs."

Each safe house had its own combination of knocks to be made on the door or window for admittance. In Harrison County, Ohio, for instance, around the town of Cadiz, the signal was three knocks. The person inside would ask, "Who's there?" and the secret reply was "A friend with friends."

Levi Coffin wrote:

> Seldom a week passed without our receiving passengers by this mysterious road. We found it necessary to be always prepared to receive such company and properly care for them. We knew not what night or what hour of the night we would be roused from slumber by a gentle rap at the door. That was the signal announcing the arrival of the Underground Railroad, for the locomotive did not whistle nor make any unnecessary noise.[13]

Since there were no telephones, and slaves did not have access to the telegraph, various signals were used to send messages between houses. In Quincy, Illinois, students from the Mission Institute School for Missionaries crossed the Mississippi River and patrolled the Missouri shore every Sunday night. They softly tapped stones together as signals. Slowly, out of the woods came cautious fugitives to be guided across the river to a "waiting room." The waiting room was actually a red barn, where they could be kept until Underground Railroad workers took them to the next stop. (The institute was eventually set on fire by a pro-slavery group from Missouri, which crossed the Mississippi when it was frozen in order to destroy the school buildings.)

Guides leading fugitives across the Ohio River used the shrill call of the hoot owl. It was known as the "river signal." General R.R. Davies recalled how he used to hear the secret hoot owl signal when he would visit his grandfather as a child:

Somehow in the night I was wakened up, and a wagon came down over the hill to the river. Then a call was given, a hoot-owl call, and this was answered by a similar one from the other side; then a boat went out and brought over the crowd. My mother got out of bed and kneeled down and prayed for them, and had me kneel with her. [14]

Lights also were used effectively as signals, because they were quiet and unobtrusive. Slaves approaching an Underground house in Ripley, Ohio, said they could see the light of the house at night guiding them to safety. Workers using boats on the Delaware River put a yellow light below a blue one. They were met some distance out from the shore by boats also showing lights in the same colors.

DISGUISES

In addition to devising secret codes, Underground Railroad workers also became very good at disguising their passengers. Men were dressed as women; women were dressed as men. Tattered clothes were exchanged for rich or modest garments. A number of accessories were used.

One of the most exciting escapes using a disguise was that of Ellen and William Craft. Ellen, a Georgia slave, was very light-skinned while her husband William was very dark. Their guide disguised Ellen as a male planter and William as her servant. The "planter" pretended to have a toothache and wrapped his face in linen to hide the fact that this planter did not shave. Green glasses hid the planter's "weak eyes." Because Ellen didn't know how to write, the guide made up the story that the planter had a sprained wrist. The couple stayed at the best hotels during their trip without being discovered and eventually made it to freedom.

In another daring escape using the element of disguise, two young slave girls had made their way from Tennessee to Indiana, where their grandparents and most of their relatives had settled in a small community called Cabin Creek. Unfortunately, their former master located them, obtained a writ for the girls' arrest, and hired a band of armed "roughs" to help him.

Meanwhile, a boy on a horse rode through the Cabin Creek neighborhood, spreading the warning that a slave hunter was in the area. When the slave hunter arrived at the cabin where the two girls were staying, the girls' grandmother seized a corn-cutter and placed herself at the cabin door. She said she would cut in two the first man who tried to cross her threshold. A crowd of some 200 black and white neighbors had gathered to watch, and the grandmother allowed neighbors to freely go in and out the cabin.

An uncle of the girls arrived and studied the writ. While he was stalling, pretending to argue over the language of the writ, the girls inside were dressed in boys' clothes. Slouch hats covered their faces. They left un-detected with several of the neighbors who were coming in and out of the house and made their getaway on two swift horses hidden in the bushes. When the uncle finally allowed the slave hunters to enter the cabin, they were furious they couldn't find the girls. The crowd taunted them and one suggested they look for a hole where the girls had been let down to the Underground Railroad.

Clothes and accessories were very important, then, in deceiving slave hunters or pro-slavery supporters. Women's groups disguised as "library associations," "reading circles," or "sewing circles" spent much of their time sewing and gathering clothes to disguise runaway slaves. The Quaker attire was a favorite because it was inconspicuous—a light gray dress and a bonnet with a heavy veil. Rich-looking clothes were also in demand because slave hunters were looking for fugitives in rags.

Some escapes involved elaborate schemes in which a disguise was a key. In 1858, for instance, a young mulatto girl was dressed in silk and ribbons. Her guides even furnished her with a borrowed white baby and a servant (played by one of the guide's daughters). The group boarded the train at the station quite safely, but imagine the fugitive's horror when she saw her former master sitting in the same car!

The escaping slave remained calm and was unnoticed for the entire trip. In Detroit, she boarded the ferry boat that would take her to freedom. Her master stood on the dock, searching the passengers, looking for his runaway. The "nurse" returned to shore with the borrowed baby just as the gangplank was raised. Much to the amusement of bystanders, the slave could not resist raising her borrowed veil and waving good-bye to her furious master.

Props were also used to provide runaways with a variety of new identities and occupations. A slave disguised as a farmer might carry a hoe, a rake, or a scythe. An Underground worker might even carry produce in baskets, pretending to be on the way to market to sell his food.

Harriet Tubman liked to pose as an old woman to disguise her athletic build, and she once used chickens as props on a rescue mission to deliver her parents out of the South. She appeared bent over, a sunbonnet pulled down over her eyes to disguise her scar, and carried a pair of chickens, legs tied together, squawking loudly.

Harriet was walking along the road toward her parents' cabin when she heard hoofbeats. As they drew near, she was horrified to see Doc Thompson, her old master—cigar in his mouth, gold watch chain dangling from his waist, broad-brimmed Panama hat covering his head—just as she had remembered him.

Harriet knew she could never outrun Thompson's

horse, so she gave a violent jerk to the string on the chickens' legs. Squawking and fluttering they took off down the road. Harriet let out a shriek and took off hobbling after them. Her former master laughed and shouted, "Go it, Granny! I'll bet on the chickens but go it anyway, Granny!"[15]

One of the most ingenious props used in Underground Railroad work was the crutch. Tar Adams, a free African-American living in Washington, Pennsylvania, actually was a very fast runner, but he went around town on crutches as a disguise. Once Tar was standing in the blacksmith shop, leaning on his crutches. He saw slave hunters ride past with the sheriff. He knew they were headed for nearby Middleton where slaves were hidden.

Tar bolted into action. He dropped his crutches and raced over the hills to warn the slaves. The sheriff recognized Tar and saw him take off. He told the slave hunters it was useless to go any further. Tar Adams would reach Middleton long before they could, using his speed and knowledge of shortcuts in the area. The slave hunters laughed at him, but when they did reach Middleton, there were no slaves to be found.

Unfortunately, not all escapes using disguises were successful. John Fairfield once contacted Levi Coffin about safely smuggling twenty-eight fugitives out of Cincinnati. It was decided they would disguise the fugitives as a funeral party. Two coaches were hired to lead the procession. The slaves would march along behind them to Cumminsville, where there was a burying ground that had a section reserved for blacks. Just beyond the burying ground, however, was a colony of black families, the group's real destination.

Fairfield decided to put the women and children into the coaches and gave them warm blankets. One woman had a very young baby, and to muffle any cries the baby might make, he, too, was wrapped tightly in a warm blanket. The funeral procession arrived safely at the colony, but when the mother unwrapped the baby, she found that he had died of suffocation.

HIDING PLACES

Once the slaves reached their destination, Underground workers also devised many ingenious ways of hiding the slaves until they could be transported to the next stop. During the 1800s many houses were larger and could offer a variety of hiding places. One design, an octagonally shaped house that was very popular in the 1850s, had networks of false walls built into the attics. Secret chambers were added to cellars. Secret doors led to closets or secret rooms. False cupboards were built over brick ovens. Sliding panels beside the fireplaces hid not wood, but fugitives.

Eli F. Brown's house in Amesville, Ohio, had a built-on addition with paneled walls. One of the panels, when manipulated, became the entrance to a secret chamber. Nathaniel Borden's house in Fall River, Massachusetts, contained a library with bookcases full of leather-bound books. When a key was turned in the lock in the front of the bookcases, however, it turned out that the books were not books at all, just false book spines. The bookcase doors swung out, revealing a ladder leading into a cellar.

Outside, a wood pile might have a room in the center; a coal bank might be hollow, or a corncrib might contain more than just food for the pigs. In Delaware, Ohio, a station keeper hid a slave woman and her child under the floor of a barn with horses trampling wheat above them. Matthew McKeever hid eight slaves in a sheep loft for four weeks, and he boasted that although he had a family of twenty on the premises, no one, not even his wife, knew he was hiding the slaves. "They were fed," he said "all that time out of our spring house and kitchen by

John Jordan (another Underground helper). There was never anything missed, only the hired girl told Mrs. McKeever somebody was stealing the bread."[16]

Haystacks concealed hiding places, sometimes reached by tunnels leading into the middle. When a slave girl in Kentucky found out that she was going to be sold, she made holes for air in a straw pile near her owner's barn. She also dug a winding passage with a concealed entrance where her fellow slaves could bring her food and water. She hid there for six weeks. The entire time she could hear her master's voice as he directed the search for his missing slave.

Wooded areas, of course, offered a variety of refuges, especially "blow-downs," places in the woods where strong winds had cut a swath through the forest, making it easy to walk through. About a mile (1.6 km) from the McKeever house was a place called Penitentiary Woods. The woods was very thick, but hidden in the center was a clearing where a cabin had been erected. Around the cabin, fields were under cultivation. These fields were worked by the escaping slaves who hid there when pursuit made it too dangerous to continue on their way. Sometimes slaves remained there through the harvest season until they could be conducted to the next station.

In towns, church belfries might hide a few runaway slaves. A schoolhouse closed down for the summer might have mysterious visitors entering at night. Slaves were hidden under the floor of a shed and the boards were nailed down over them. A gristmill, a brick kiln, or any building could become a hiding place for desperate runaways.

USING SUBTERFUGE

Most Underground Railroad workers were moral, upstanding members of their communities. They did not like breaking the law, but felt it necessary for the freedom of black men and women. They did not like to lie, but would if necessary. Many developed ways of tricking the "enemy" to get around these moral dilemmas.

A tavern keeper of Bloomfield, Ohio, for instance, took in a fugitive couple and their three children, fed them, then put them in the charge of a conductor. That night, the slaves' owner, his son, and a slave catcher arrived, demanding to know where their slaves were. The tavern keeper talked them into spending the night.

Somehow the next morning, the slave catchers overslept. Breakfast was slow in coming. The grooms were slow in getting the horses ready. The stable door key had been left in the house and it took ten minutes to find it. One of the horses had lost a shoe and the blacksmith's shop was locked. No one knew where the blacksmith was. When he was found, he had no nails or shoes. It was nearly noon by the time the furious slave owner and his group left. By then the fugitives were well on their way.

Another time, John and Mary Smith were hiding two women fugitives when some slaveholders arrived. While John answered the door, Mary took the girls into the bedchamber, pulled the bed apart, lifted the mattress, and whispered for the girls to lie down on the ropes that supported the mattress. Mrs. Smith remade the bed over the girls and went downstairs.

"Let them come in, John," she told her husband. "Thee knows there are no slaves here."[17]

Mrs. Smith had not lied in her mind. To the Quaker, there was no such thing as a slave.

And so, Underground Railroad workers waged their war on slavery—not with uniforms, but with disguises, not with tents, but with corncribs and haystacks, not with bullets, but with words.

SEVEN
GETTING SETTLED

*After the Fugitive Law took effect, the runaways came there
[to Canada] by fifties every day, like frogs in Egypt.* [1]
*—Anthony Bingey, an escaped slave who helped
fugitives in Amherstburg, Ontario*

The slaves' troubles were not over once they escaped.
They found that adapting to a new home could be very
difficult. Most had been fed, clothed, and cared for on
their plantations—sometimes since birth. They had never
had to fend for themselves, never had to find their own
shelter, food, or clothing. Suddenly, survival was a
frightening prospect.

FUGITIVE COMMUNITIES

A lucky slave might come across other fugitive slaves in
hiding and form a community. From Virginia to North
Carolina large groups of runaway slaves built huts and
farmed on hidden islands where few white men dared to
follow. They made small items like barrel staves or
shingles to trade for salted provisions, coarse clothes, and
tools offered by a group of traders known as "swamp
merchants," so-called because they peddled their wares in
the swamp. Some of these exiles became known as
"maroons," from the Spanish *cimarron,* meaning wild. It
was estimated that eventually 2,000 maroons were living
in Virginia at one time; some had been born in the
swamp and had never even seen a white man!

Some runaways found safety among certain Native
American tribes despite threats from white people or

rewards offered for their return. Towns consisting of fugitives inside Indian territory existed in the Carolinas and Georgia before 1812. The Seminoles, particularly, had the reputation for treating the slaves well, and instances of intermarriages between slaves and Indians were well known. In 1835, in fact, President Andrew Jackson sent troops to Florida to relocate the Seminoles to an area beyond the Mississippi. Jackson told the tribe that no blacks, including half- or quarter-breeds living with the Seminoles could go with them when they moved. The Seminoles refused to leave without the blacks in their care and it was one of the reasons Chief Osceola began the Second Seminole War (1835–1842).*

FUGITIVES IN THE NORTH

After fugitives reached safety in the North, some encountered black communities or relatives who had escaped before them. Others eventually found employment and disappeared into the crowded cities and towns. Some settled where Quakers and other religious groups assured them safety. Large settlements of African-Americans grew in places such as Greenwich, New Jersey; Columbus and Akron, Ohio; Elmira and Buffalo, New York; and Detroit, Michigan.

When the Civil War began, many fugitives, as well as freed Negroes, found shelter and work with the Union army. Some blacks, among them Harriet Tubman, helped northern spies by providing information on roads and unmarked trails in southern areas. They had lots of practice in keeping secrets and used what they had learned on the Underground Railroad. They taught Union soldiers how to use the same swamps, the same woods, and the North Star they had used to escape. In

*The Seminoles had agreed, in 1832, to move west of the Mississippi, but before they could do so, Chief Osceola and his tribe revolted in 1835. Osceola was captured in 1837 under a flag of truce, but the war continued without him until 1842.

return, the Union army fed, sheltered, and protected these ex-slaves from recapture.

Those who did not have government help found the freedom they had sought so eagerly had its pitfalls. Some thought that they would live a life of leisure like some of the white men and women they saw. But reality was harsh. Soon some of them were dying from exposure because they had no shelter, or from starving because they had no food. They soon learned that freedom did not mean freedom from work.

For those who had worked the plantations, the most obvious choice of work in the North was farming. They found jobs as general field laborers, raised crops for landlords, and some even became tenant farmers—farmers who rented the land to produce crops for the market. A few banded together and formed cooperative groups to farm the land together and share the profits.

Those who had been artisans or skilled workers on the plantations looked for similar work in the cities. They became mechanics, bricklayers, blacksmiths, carpenters, wheelwrights, and masons. Many worked in factories, mines, or lumber mills. Some worked on building the new railroads that were soon to crisscross the nation.

Those who had been house slaves found work as domestic servants with northern families. Others worked in hotels as waiters, chambermaids, valets, or nurses.

A few of the fugitives arrived with funds and quickly saw that the way to independence was in owning a business. They kept stalls in the market where they sold fruits, candies, cakes, and lemonade. They went into oystering or other small fishing businesses on the coast. They opened small shops. For some, these small businesses grew and grew, becoming big businesses worth thousands, and in a few cases, millions of dollars. Several ex-fugitives became the wealthiest people in the neighborhood.

For the vast majority, however, this new experience of having money all to themselves was a heady, sometimes confusing experience. Many could not read or write and so they did not understand the contracts or legal obligations that working involved. Many had no idea how much things cost and greedy merchants quickly took advantage of them, charging them sometimes ten times as much as they charged white people. They did not understand the concept of credit and quickly got deeply into debt. Instead of healthy food, some spent their money on luxury items like sardines, potted meats and canned goods, and fruit out of season. Instead of sensible clothes, they were attracted to bright, gaudy, costly items. And many discovered one of the biggest evils of freedom – alcohol.

They also found that despite the fact that they were free in the North, this did not mean they were free from prejudice. They suffered taunts, name-calling, even beatings at the hands of those who still believed in slavery. They were barred from many places, including eating places, cabins on steamers, and even religious revival meetings.

Immigrants, especially, felt that the newly arrived fugitives were taking jobs that should have been theirs. They often protested and even violently attacked blacks. Congressman Cadwallader C. Washburn of Wisconsin said of the escaped slave, "Because he is so out of place [in the North], we propose keeping him out of the free Territories and not allowing him, with his unpaid labor, to come in contact with white men and white labor."[2]

One of the biggest problems for the ex-fugitives who flocked to the North was finding shelter. Those lucky enough to find employment on farms had their shelter provided for them or built log cabins with mud chimneys similar to those found on southern plantations. These tiny, single-room dwellings had wood shingle roofs and square holes for windows. The windows were protected with shutters or patches of old clothing or newspapers. The family slept on the floor in front of the fireplace.

Those who remained in the cities found shelter with

fellow blacks. They might live in a one-room shanty with twelve to twenty other people. These shanties often had leaky roofs and no furniture. The residents slept on dirt floors with wood blocks for pillows. They ate standing inside or out. There was no security, no privacy, and no dignity in these houses. However, others were not even that lucky. They lived in deserted, ruined houses or built huts from leftover lumber they scrounged. Some lived like vagrants—under sheds, under bridges, and in caves.

Because of the lack of shelter from the harsh northern winters or the crowded conditions of the shacks they lived in, and because of a lack of knowledge of health practices and failure to carry out doctors' suggestions, the mortality rate among Negroes was extremely high. According to partial census reports for 1865–1866, more Negroes died from disease than white people were killed in the Civil War. Children were espesially vulnerable. In 1868, for example, 136 white children died; that year three times as many Negro children died—a stunning 372. [3]

For many, the realization soon dawned that the only way to stem the tide of deaths was through education. The only way to fulfill that lifelong dream of becoming a preacher or teacher was through education. As the fugitives settled in the community, the organizations who were trying to provide shelter, food, and medical care were swamped with requests for help in learning to read and write.

Organizations and individuals quickly set about providing schools. Soon, "refined and delicate" ladies were volunteering for organizations such as the Boston Education Society or Port Royal Society of Philadelphia that specialized in educating the fugitives. Negro troops in the Union armies gave instruction to the newly arrived fugitives and during their free time, ex-slaves could be seen poring over readers and textbooks. Government agencies took over abandoned properties and set up schoolhouses, furnishing them with teachers, books, and school furniture. Soon the North was covered with black

106

Emancipation carried a heavy price, as many blacks
discovered when they faced tremendous economic and
social hardships following the Civil War.

day and night schools, industrial schools, Sunday schools, and even colleges.

The schools knew no age limit as far as the pupils were concerned. Parents and children sat side by side, fingers earnestly moving along the confusing new words. One observer wrote:

> In one which I examined, the dux [leader] was a quick bright-eyed little boy of seven, next to whom came a great hulking Negro of six feet [1.8 m] or above, who had been a plantation slave for nearly twenty years, [and] next to him came a little girl, then a buxom woman, then another child or two, then another man, and so on, giving the class a very grotesque look. Oldest of all, an elderly Negro, who stood with an earnest face at the foot of the class turned out to be the father of the little fellow at the top.[4]

The teachers who worked with the fugitives were constantly amazed at the enthusiasm and quickness of their new students. Although some gave up or lost interest, for many of the students, school was like playtime. They often came to school after a hard day's work, and some might have traveled through snow or pelting rain to get there. To not be able to go to school would be a severe punishment for many fugitives. In fact, it is said that when one school was threatened with closure, the authorities received a petition containing 10,000 signatures (many of them a simple X) begging to keep the school open. Some former slaves even offered to pay out of their own meager funds.

FUGITIVES IN CANADA

Thousands of fugitives did not stop in the northern states. Instead, they continued on to Canada where they formed huge settlements of African-Americans. Many of these settlements were formed near the border because

108

the fugitives were out of money, or they wanted to stay close to the United States in case they decided to return to relatives and family. Some stayed close to the border because the soil was similar to that of the United States. Settlements were quickly founded at towns such as Welland, St. Catherines, and Hamilton, near Niagara Falls; at Colchester, Windsor, and Amherstburg across from Detroit; and at London, Chatham, and Dresden near Lake Erie.

Places that held Underground Railroad terminals also had large black populations. Nova Scotia had a black population of about 12 percent and towns like Lincolnville, Tracadie, Milford Haven, and Boylston still have black residents who can trace their roots to escapees on the Underground Railroad. One huge settlement known as the Queen's Bush, southwest of Toronto, stretched as far as Lake Huron.

One of the biggest and most organized settlements of fugitives was known first as the British-American Institute and then as the Dawn Settlement. The ex-slave, Josiah Henson, began the settlement with just fifty blacks. It soon expanded to 400 white, Indian, and black settlers. It was designed to be a manual labor school to teach boys and girls manual and domestic arts like blacksmithing and sewing. It would be a place to provide shelter until the fugitives "could be placed out upon the wild lands in the neighborhoods to earn their own subsistence."[5]

Another successful settlement for fugitives was called Elgin and was located in Buxton, Canada. Here land was parceled into 50-acre farms at the price of $2.50 per acre. The organizer, the Rev. William King, provided a model of a small log house and instructed those wishing to live in the settlement to build their houses just like the model. By 1862, there were more than a thousand people living in about 200 of the little log houses. It became a typical example of black settlements built in Canada during that time.

The fugitives who sought refuge in Canadian cities

and towns soon found conditions similar to those in the United States. Prejudice also existed in Canada, much to their disappointment. Education was available, but some schools were segregated or the black students had to "occupy a seat set apart" in white schools. Many churches made Negroes sit in a back gallery which they called "Nigger heaven." One visitor in 1848 noticed Negroes lived "in the least valuable corner of the towns," and like the immigrants in the United States, Canadians worried about the fugitives taking jobs that should have been theirs, or that they would soon take over the country. A Toronto newspaper editorial in 1851 complained that

> .... Already we have a far greater number of negroes in the province than the good of the country requires, and we would suggest the propriety of levying a poll tax on all who may come to us for the future. ... We abhor slavery, but patriotism induces us to exclaim against having our country overrun by blacks, many of whom are woefully depraved by their previous mode of life.[6]

Also, just as those Negroes struggled to find housing and jobs in the North, many struggled in Canada. However, the Candian government was offering vast amounts of land to settlers willing to clear it and farm it and these farmers desperately needed help. The fugitives filled this need. They, in turn, were encouraged to settle on government land and become farmers. Many were sold homesteads—government land that had been divided into 50-acre lots and which sold for two dollars an acre. The homesteaders had ten years to pay for the land, and they received a clear title once the land was paid for.

Other fugitives found a variety of jobs in Canadian cities. In addition to taking jobs similar to those found in the United States, some worked in hotels or as tour guides at Niagara Falls. Black merchants included barrel makers, restaurant owners, and shopkeepers who made and sold rope, dresses, wigs, and other necessities. Lemon John sold his special ice cream on the streets of Toronto, and Nathan S. Powell sold Powell's Indian Tonic in Colchester. In Bronte, the first blacksmith shop was opened by a black fugitive. In Saint John, the city's ice trade was owned and operated by a black, Robert Whetsel. Another black, Joseph Mink, became wealthy operating a line of stagecoaches. New Brunswick even had a black hangman.

For the less successful arrivals, organizations were founded to help them find food, shelter, and work. Missions handled "fugitive goods," large boxes of clothing and bedding sent from the United States. Schools such as the British and American Manual Labor Institute for Colored Children were created. Self-improvement societies were organized to improve education and help stop begging among the starving newcomers.

Underground Railroad workers from the United States often kept in contact with their "ex-passengers" or visited Canada to see how they were making out. Elizabeth Buffum Chace of Valley Falls, Rhode Island, often gave fugitives stamped envelopes to mail when they reached their destination. Levi Coffin made several trips into Canada to visit with his successes. He ate with them, stayed with them overnight, prayed with them, and was kissed and cried over. Children were held up to him to be admired. He and others found that despite the hardships, few slaves yearned for their old life. As one former slave told Levi Coffin, speaking of his one-year-old son, "We can call him our own; old master can not take him from us and sell him."[7]

EIGHT
END OF THE LINE

The war came a little too soon for my business. I
wanted to help off three thousand slaves. I had only
got up to twenty-seven hundred.
—Thomas Garrett, when the Civil War ended his
activities in the Underground Railroad[1]

The Underground Railroad ended as informally as it had
begun; it just slowly ceased to exist. By May 1861, a
month after the firing on Fort Sumter and the start of the
Civil War, fugitives were coming across the borders in
carloads. The Fugitive Slave Law was still in existence, but
the Underground Railroad no longer had to work in
secret and it was not necessary to take the fugitives all the
way to Canada.

Hiding places that had saved the fugitives were put to
other uses or preserved as curiosities to show to small
children. Stories of great escapes and fantastic bravery
would be told by word of mouth because of the lack of
written records. (And they often became more exaggerated with each telling.) The tracks of the Underground
Railroad were abandoned because there was no more
traffic. The stations were closed because there were no
more travelers.

As the Fredonia, New York, newspaper, *Censor,* noted
on November 18, 1868:

> ...this celebrated company is now broken up,
> and its business will never be resuscitated.
> President Lincoln, by proclamation, took away
> all the transportation, and rendered the stock
> worthless. Gen. Grant and the "Boys in Blue"

tore up the track and destroyed the structure, so that it will never be used again. ...What would appear singular with most companies, the stockholders do not mourn over their loss. [2]

ECONOMIC EFFECTS

In the years the Underground Railroad was active, from the 1840s to 1863, the enormous economic losses the Underground Railroad caused would become legend—thousands of humans sent to freedom, each of them representing an investment of about $700 to $2,000. It is impossible to calculate any real figures of financial losses, however, because of the lack of national figures.

Some figures were gathered from congressional meetings where southern congressmen complained about huge losses caused by the Underground Railroad. As early as 1822, Congressman Moore of Virginia told the House that his district lost four or five thousand dollars every year. Others gave estimates of $80,000, $100,000 and even $200,000. Congressman Clingman of North Carolina said the fugitives living in the North were worth about $15,000,000. While most people believed these reports were exaggerated, they do show that losses were taking place and that the southerners were upset about these losses.

It is also impossible to estimate the number of slaves who were transported by the Underground Railroad or even the number who escaped by themselves. The fugitives were not anxious to make themselves known by participating in statistical surveys such as the census.

When census figures were available, they were often woefully inadequate. Some believe this may have been because of the way they divided citizens into racial groups; others believe it was through ignorance of government procedures on the part of those surveyed.

For instance, the census for 1850 states only 1,011 slaves escaped. In 1860, only 803 slaves escaped, according to census figures. If this is so, ask historians, why did southerners complain so loudly in Congress about their losses and continually ask for more stringent laws? Why do these figures differ so greatly from those provided by the slave owners? Why do they differ so greatly from those provided later by Underground Railroad workers?

While Underground Railroad workers did not usually keep statistics on paper because of the danger involved, they did vocally offer numbers that disagree greatly with census estimates. And those few who did keep records also differed. For instance, a diary kept by Daniel Osborn, a Quaker in Alum Creek Settlement, an Ohio Underground Railroad station, included a record of every black passing through his neighborhood from April 14 to September 10, 1844. Osborn's diary indicated forty-seven fugitives escaped in just those few months. Robert Purvis of Philadelphia kept a record of the fugitives who were helped by the Vigilance Committee of Philadelphia. He estimated that the society helped at least one slave a day. From 1830 to 1860, therefore, they would have helped more than 9,000 blacks escape.

SOCIAL EFFECTS

Although the Underground Railroad was not responsible for the Civil War, it is believed that the vast number of slaves that were helped to freedom, augmented by the huge economic losses the South suffered, escalated the possibility of war. It is also believed by some that the Underground Railroad also helped slave owners by eliminating insurrections.

Terrible insurrections, or rebellions, had taken place in San Domingo from 1791 to 1793 and three occurred in the United States—in 1800, 1820, and 1831. There was always the fear among plantation owners that it would happen again. One black historian, George W. Williams, in his book *History of the Negro Race in America,* says the Underground Railroad provided "a safety valve to the institution of slavery. As soon as leaders arose among the slaves who refused to endure the yoke, they would go North. Had they remained, there might have been enacted at the South the direful scenes of San Domingo."[3]

In principal, the Underground Railroad was effective as a protest against slavery. Large numbers of people banded together to help the oppressed. In a roundabout way, they also punished the oppressors. Large numbers of people banded together to defy laws that they had long found unjust. It was a way of bringing the horrors of slavery to the attention of many people who knew nothing about it. It was a way of convincing the South that antislavery people meant business.

And it was a way an everyday person could become an adventurer. Albert Bushnell Hart, a professor of history at Harvard University said in 1898:

> Above all, the Underground Railroad was the opportunity for the bold and adventurous, it had the excitement of piracy, the secrecy of burglary, the daring of insurrection; to the pleasure of relieving the poor negros' sufferings it added the triumph of snapping one's fingers at the slave catcher.[4]

THE END OF THE UNDERGROUND RAILROAD

The Underground Railroad ended when President Abraham Lincoln signed the Emancipation Proclamation. The proclamation stated "...That on the first day of January in the year of our Lord one thousand eight hundred and sixty-three, all persons held as slaves within any State...shall be thenceforth and forever free...."[5]

Although the proclamation did not end slavery immediately, it was a powerful beginning. Lincoln said, "All that I can say now is that I believe the proclamation has knocked the bottom out of slavery, though at no time have I expected any sudden results out of it."[6]

There was rejoicing not only throughout the United States, but in England and Canada as well. In London, several thousand workers set aside New Year's Eve, 1862, when the proclamation would take effect, as a "watch night," a night to denounce slavery. In the northern United States, a watch night was planned in black churches. Lights were placed in windows and church members sat silently remembering the passengers, the conductors, the stationmasters—the heroes and heroines of the Underground Railroad. Others mourned for the untold numbers who died in the quest for freedom.

On New Year's Eve, Harriet Beecher Stowe entered her church, a shabby little figure, bonnet slightly askew, eyes filled with tears. The whole audience rose to its feet for the "little woman who started this great war." Through the cheers came the sound of the clock striking midnight. As the chimes died, a vast silence descended over the church. One by one, black and white, the watchers joined hands and a jubilant hymn filled the air. It was a start.

GLOSSARY

abolition–the legal extinction of Negro slavery

Abolition Society–an organization dedicated to putting an end to the enslavement of Negroes

baliwork (or bailiwick)–a district or place under the jurisdiction of a bailie or bailiff (authority)

blow down–an area laid bare by winds traveling through a woods or forest

brick kiln–a furnace or oven for burning, baking, or drying something

chain gang–a group of prisoners chained together while they work

chattels–moveable property, including slaves

Congregationalists–a Puritan religious sect whose members tended to believe the government of the church should be managed by the members of the church or congregation. Social service was the main aim of the church.

corn crib–a small structure used to store corn before shelling. It has slats for ventilation and is elevated off the ground to keep insects off the corn.

covenanters–members of a Presbyterian religious sect of Scottish origin. Covenanters believed they had signed an agreement with God and rejected the divine right of kings. They believed more in the rights of the people.

effigy–the image of a person. Usually an effigy was made and then burned or hanged to represent hostility.

fugitive–a person who flees; a runaway

Fugitive Slave Laws–a number of laws that regulated the return of slaves who had escaped

gallows–a wooden frame made up of a cross beam on two uprights on which condemned people were hanged

117

gaoling—putting in jail

grist mill—a building with machinery for grinding grain for many customers at once

guilders—a gold or silver coin minted in the Netherlands, Germany, or Austria and used in the United States by newcomers from these countries before American currency was minted

hackman—the driver of a coach or carriage

haycock—a pile of hay shaped like a cone. It was used for drying the hay after mowing.

indenture—a law or written agreement binding one person to work for another for a given length of time

kearsey (or kersey)—a British term for a woolen fabric with a highly lustrous fine nap. The word was derived from the English town of Kersey where it was made. (Nap is the downy or hairy surface of cloth.)

linsey (or lindsey)—a coarse, loosely woven fabric made of linen and wool. The word is derived from Linsey, a village in Sussex, England where the fabric was first made.

manumitted—released from slavery; freed

mulatto—a person who has one Negro parent and one white

Negro house—a house where Negroes could be hidden from harm

overseer—the person in charge of supervising work on a plantation

plantation system—the economic system where crops are planted and cultivated on large areas of land

posse—a group of people temporarily organized to conduct a search

Quakers—the term used to describe members of a religion called the Society of Friends. It was first used by George Fox, the founder of the religion, who told the members of the church to "tremble at the word of the Lord."

safe houses—a term used by the Underground Railroad to

118

describe houses belonging to people involved in helping Negro slaves to escape

skiff—a boat small enough for sailing or rowing by one person

Society of Friends—religion founded by George Fox about 1650. Friends were known to be opposed to taking oaths and to war.

subterfuge—a plan or action used to escape or evade a person or situation

Underground superintendent—the head of a certain section of the Underground Railroad

writ—a formal order issued in the name of a court or government that the person to whom it is addressed stop or do some specified act

SOURCE NOTES

CHAPTER ONE: THE CONFLICT BEGINS

1. Quoted in Wilbur Siebert, *The Underground Railroad* (New York: Russell and Russell, 1898), p. 196.
2. Quoted in Henrietta Buckmaster, *Let My People Go* (New York: Harper and Brothers, 1941), p. 19.
3. Mary Stoughton Locke, *Anti-Slavery in America* (Gloucester, Mass.: Peter Smith, 1965), p. 15.
4. Ibid.
5. Siebert, *The Underground Railroad,* p. 92.
6. Earle A. Forrest, "Slavery in Washington County," *History of Washington County* (Chicago: The S.J. Clarke Publishing Co., 1926), p. 411.
7. Ann Petry, *Harriet Tubman* (New York: Pocket Books, 1955), p. 160.
8. Larry Gara, *The Liberty Line* (Lexington: University of Kentucky Press, 1961), p. 23.
9. Locke, *Anti-Slavery in America,* p. 24.
10. Ibid., p. 44.
11. Siebert, *The Underground Railroad,* p. 93.
12. Locke, *Anti-Slavery in America,* p. 23.
13. Ibid., p. 31.

CHAPTER TWO: LAYING THE TRACKS TO FREEDOM

1. John Greenleaf Whittier, *Poetical Works* (Boston: Houghton Mifflin, 1975), p. 297.
2. Forrest, "Slavery in Washington County," p. 418.
3. Locke, *Anti-Slavery in America,* p. 189.
4. Siebert, *The Underground Railroad* p. 45.
5. Gara, *The Liberty Line,* p. 173.
6. Petry, *Harriet Tubman,* p. 134.
7. Siebert, *The Underground Railroad* p. 322.
8. Ibid., p. 323.

9. Ibid., p. 249.

CHAPTER THREE: WORKING ON THE RAILROAD

1. Buckmaster, *Let My People Go,* p. 37.
2. Levi Coffin, *Reminiscences of Levi Coffin* (New York: Arno Press and the New York Times, 1968), p. 432.
3. Ibid., p. 445.
4. Ibid., p. 443.
5. Forrest, "Slavery in Washington County," p. 424.
6. Coffin, *Reminiscenses of Levi Coffin,* pp. 12–13.
7. Buckmaster, *Let My People Go,* pp. 78–79.
8. Quoted in Siebert, *The Underground Railroad,* p. 104.
9. Petry, *Harriet Tubman,* p. 92.
10. Ibid., p. 158.
11. Ibid., pp. 150–51.
12. Ibid., pp. 150–51.
13. Ibid., p. 221.
14. William Breyfogle, *Make Free* (Philadelphia: J.B. Lippincott Company, 1958), p. 178.

CHAPTER FOUR: THE HARDSHIPS OF RAILROAD WORK

1. Siebert, *The Underground Railroad,* pp. 109–110.
2. Gara, *The Liberty Line,* p. 150.
3. Ibid.
4. Ibid, p. 158.
5. Ibid.
6. Ibid., pp. 73–74.
7. Breyfogle, *Make Free,* p. 178.
8. Quoted in Forrest, "Slavery in Washington County," p. 414.
9. Gara, *The Liberty Line,* p. 72.
10. Coffin, *Reminiscences of Levi Coffin,* p. 117.
11. Buckmaster, *Let My People Go,* p. 90.
12. Ibid., p. 103.
13. Siebert, *The Underground Railroad,* p. 169.

CHAPTER FIVE: RIDING THE RAILS TO FREEDOM

1. Dwight Lowell Dumond, *Anti-Slavery: The Crusade for Freedom in America* (Ann Arbor: University of Michigan, 1961), p. 310.
2. Buckmaster, *Let My People Go,* p. 68.

3. Quoted in Siebert, *The Underground Railroad,* p. 160.
4. Forrest, "Slavery in Washington County," p. 426.
5. Coffin, *Reminiscences of Levi Coffin,* p. 99.
6. Gara, *The Liberty Line,* p. 52.
7. William Still, *The Underground Railroad* (Chicago: Johnson Company, 1970), p. 68.
8. Richard O. Boyer, *The Legend of John Brown* (New York: Alfred A. Knopf, 1973), p. 404.
9. Ibid.
10. Coffin, *Reminiscences of Levi Coffin,* p. 439.

CHAPTER SIX: THE ART OF
"TRAVELING THE RAILS"
1. Siebert, *The Underground Railroad,* p. 310.
2. Gara, *The Liberty Line,* p. 36.
3. Ibid.
4. Ibid., p. 144.
5. Ibid.
6. Ibid., p. 146.
7. Ibid., p. 149.
8. Ibid., p. 147.
9. Siebert, *The Underground Railroad* p. 58.
10. Buckmaster, *Let My People Go,* p. 150.
11. Coffin, *Reminiscences of Levi Coffin,* pp. 454–55.
12. Petry, *Harriet Tubman,* pp. 136–37.
13. Coffin, *Reminiscences of Levi Coffin,* p. 112.
14. Siebert, *The Underground Railroad,* p. 56.
15. Petry, *Harriet Tubman.* pp. 168–69.
16. Forrest, "Slavery in Washington County," p. 426.
17. Buckmaster, *Let My People Go,* p. 30.

CHAPTER SEVEN: GETTING SETTLED
1. Siebert, *The Underground Railroad,* p. 249.
2. Gara, *The Liberty Line,* p. 63.
3. Donald Henderson, *The Negro Freedman* (New York: Henry Schuman, 1952), p. 154.
4. Ibid., p. 99.
5. Siebert, *The Underground Railroad,* p. 206.
6. Gara, *The Liberty Line,* p. 66.
7. Coffin, *Reminiscences of Levi Coffin,* p. 186.

CHAPTER EIGHT: END OF THE LINE

1. Siebert, *The Underground Railroad,* p. 111.
2. Quoted in Ebert M. Pettit, *Sketches in the History of the Underground Railroad* (New York: Books for Libraries Press, 1971), p. 173.
3. Quoted in Siebert, *The Underground Railroad* p. 340.
4. Ibid., p. viii.
5. Quoted in Buckmaster, *Let My People Go,* pp. 300–301.
6. Ibid., pp. 306–7.

BIBLIOGRAPHY

Blockson, Charles. *The Underground Railroad*. New York: Prentice Hall, 1987.

Boyer, Richard. *The Legend of John Brown*. New York: Alfred A. Knopf, 1973.

Breyfogle, William. *Make Free*. Philadelphia: J.B. Lippincott Company, 1958.

Buckmaster, Henrietta. *Let My People Go*. New York: Harper & Brothers, 1941.

Cockrum, Col. William. *History of the Underground Railroad*. Oakland City, Ind.: J.W. Cockrum Printing Company, 1945.

Coffin, Levi. *Reminiscences of Levi Coffin*. New York: Arno Press and the New York Times, 1968.

Donald, Henderson. *The Negro Freedman*. New York: Henry Schuman, 1952.

Dubois, W.E. Burghardt. *John Brown*. New York: International Publishers, 1974.

Dumond, Dwight Lowell. *Antislavery: The Crusade for Freedom in America*. Ann Arbor, Michigan: University of Michigan Press, 1961.

Forrest, Earle A. "Slavery in Washington County," *History of Washington County*. Chicago: The S.J. Clarke Publishing Company, 1926.

Gara, Larry. *The Liberty Line*. Lexington: University of Kentucky Press, 1961.

Haviland, Laura S. *A Woman's Life-Work: Labors and Experiences of Laura S. Haviland*. Chicago: C.U. Waite and Company, 1887.

Khan, Lurey. *One Day Levin . . . He Be Free*. New York: E.P. Dutton and Company, 1972.

Locke, Mary Stoughton. *Anti-Slavery in America*. Gloucester, Mass.: Peter Smith, 1965.

Petry, Ann. *Harriet Tubman*. New York: Pocket Books, 1955.

Pettit, Ebert M. *Sketches in the History of the Underground Railroad*. New York: Books for Libraries Press, 1971.

Siebert, Wilbur. *The Underground Railroad*. New York: Russell and Russell, 1898.

Smedley, R.C. *History of the Underground Railroad in Chester and the Neighboring Counties of Pennsylvania*. Lancester, Pa.: Office of the *Journal*, 1883.

Still, William. *The Underground Railroad*. Chicago: Johnson Company, 1970.

Strother, Horatio T. *The Underground Railroad in Connecticut*. Middletown, Conn.: Wesleyan University Press, 1962.

Whitman, Walt. *Leaves of Grass*. New York: W.W. Norton & Company, 1970.

Whittier, John Greenleaf. *The Poetical Works of Whittier.* New York: Houghton Mifflin Co., 1975.

Winks, Robin W. *The Blacks in Canada*. Montreal: McGill-Queen's University Press and New Haven: Yale University Press, 1971.

INDEX

Slaves
  desire for freedom by, 17, 19
  knowledge of, 85–86
  runaway. *See* Runaway slaves
  value of, 22
Society of Friends. *See* Quakers
Still, William, 42, 46, 47, 74
Stowe, Harriet Beecher, 28–30,
  116
Subterfuge, 100–101
Surface lines, 82

Tappan, Lewis, 59
Tubman, Harriet, 38, 43, 45–49,
  78, 91, 97–98, 103

*Uncle Tom's Cabin, or Life Among
  the Lowly* (Stowe), 28–31, 72, 73
Underground Railroad
  beginning of, 21, 26, 31
  disguises used by, 83, 95–99
  economic effects of, 113–114
  end of, 112–113, 115–116
  hazards of working for, 52–62
  hiding places used by, 99–100
  opposition to, 50–51
  organization and methods
    of, 32–33, 63–65
  people active in, 33–49. *See
    also* individual names
  routes used by, 65–69, 71–84
  secret codes used by, 89–95
  social effects of, 114–115
  success of, 86–89
  use of subterfuge by, 100–101
Underground superintendent, 87
Union army, 103–104

Washburn, Cadwallader C., 105
Washington, George, 9, 19
Waterway routes, 71–78
Whitney, Eli, 22
Williams, George W., 115
Wilson, Eliza, 74–75